麦格希 中英双语阅读文库

成长的烦恼

第4辑

【美】富尔顿 (Fulton, L) ●主编

刘慧　王仲生 ●译

麦格希中英双语阅读文库编委会 ●编

全国百佳图书出版单位
吉林出版集团股份有限公司

图书在版编目（CIP）数据

成长的烦恼. 第4辑 / (美) 富尔顿 (Fulton, L) 主编；刘慧，王仲生译；麦格希中英双语阅读文库编委会编. -- 2版. -- 长春：吉林出版集团股份有限公司，2018.3（2022.1重印）
（麦格希中英双语阅读文库）
ISBN 978-7-5581-4761-6

Ⅰ.①成… Ⅱ.①富…②刘…③王…④麦… Ⅲ.①英语—汉语—对照读物②故事—作品集—美国—现代 Ⅳ.①H319.4：I

中国版本图书馆CIP数据核字(2018)第046403号

成长的烦恼　第4辑

编　　　　：	麦格希中英双语阅读文库编委会
插　　画：	齐　航　李延霞
责任编辑：	沈丽娟
封面设计：	冯冯翼
开　　本：	660mm×960mm　1/16
字　　数：	209千字
印　　张：	9.25
版　　次：	2018年3月第2版
印　　次：	2022年1月第2次印刷

出　　版：	吉林出版集团股份有限公司
发　　行：	吉林出版集团外语教育有限公司
地　　址：	长春市福祉大路5788号龙腾国际大厦B座7层
电　　话：	总编办：0431-81629929
	发行部：0431-81629927　0431-81629921(Fax)
印　　刷：	北京一鑫印务有限责任公司

ISBN 978-7-5581-4761-6　　定价：35.00元
版权所有　　侵权必究　　举报电话：0431-81629929

前言 PREFACE

英国思想家培根说过：阅读使人深刻。阅读的真正目的是获取信息，开拓视野和陶冶情操。从语言学习的角度来说，学习语言若没有大量阅读就如隔靴搔痒，因为阅读中的语言是最丰富、最灵活、最具表现力、最符合生活情景的，同时读物中的情节、故事引人入胜，进而能充分调动读者的阅读兴趣，培养读者的文学修养，至此，语言的学习水到渠成。

"麦格希中英双语阅读文库"在世界范围内选材，涉及科普、社会文化、文学名著、传奇故事、成长励志等多个系列，充分满足英语学习者课外阅读之所需，在阅读中学习英语、提高能力。

◎难度适中

本套图书充分照顾读者的英语学习阶段和水平，从读者的阅读兴趣出发，以难易适中的英语语言为立足点，选材精心、编排合理。

◎精品荟萃

本套图书注重经典阅读与实用阅读并举。既包含国内外脍炙人口、耳熟能详的美文，又包含科普、人文、故事、励志类等多学科的精彩文章。

◎功能实用

本套图书充分体现了双语阅读的功能和优势，充分考虑到读者课外阅读的方便，超出核心词表的词汇均出现在使其意义明显的语境之中，并标注释义。

鉴于编者水平有限，凡不周之处，谬误之处，皆欢迎批评教正。

我们真心地希望本套图书承载的文化知识和英语阅读的策略对提高读者的英语著作欣赏水平和英语运用能力有所裨益。

丛书编委会

Contents

Noise in the Night
夜晚的响声 / 1

Sammy Stuffit
萨米——东西控 / 8

The Footprint
脚印 / 17

Walking in Rome Footsteps
走入罗马的台阶 / 30

Neighborhood Mystery
街区秘密 / 40

The Black Stones
黑石记 / 52

Only One Aunt Maggie
只有一个玛姬姨妈 / 74

The Ant in the Photograph
照片里的蚂蚁 / 90

Carlos's Puzzle
卡洛斯的迷宫 / 104

The Mind Game
头脑游戏 / 120

Ants in My Bed
床上的蚂蚁 / 126

Noise in the Night

Manuel and Jason put up a *tent* in Manuel's yard. They put it next to the woods. They put it under a large *oak* tree.

All day long Manuel and Jason played in the tent. All week long they played in the tent. They loved playing in the tent more than anyplace else they could think of.

They took *sandwiches* to the tent and ate their lunch there.

They took games to the tent and played games there.

夜晚的响声

曼纽尔和贾森在曼纽尔的院子里搭了一个帐篷，正好旁边是树林，在一棵大橡树下面。

曼纽尔和贾森整天都在帐篷里玩耍，他们整周在帐篷里玩耍，他们喜欢在这里玩胜过他们能想起来的任何地方。

他们把三明治带到帐篷里，在那里吃午餐。

他们把玩具带到帐篷里，在那里玩玩具。

---

tent *n.* 帐篷
sandwich *n.* 三明治

oak *n.* 橡树

GROWING PAINS IV

NOISE IN THE NIGHT

They took their radio to the tent and listened to music.

Manuel and Jason read books in the tent. They brought their *favorite* toys to the tent. They brought their friends to the tent. And their friends brought their pets to the tent.

They liked being in the tent more than anything else. They only left the tent to go to their houses to eat dinner and to sleep. After an early *breakfast*, they were back in the tent.

One day they asked their parents if they could sleep in the tent. Manuel's parents said it was okay. Jason's parents also said it was okay, but only if Jason's dad slept in a tent next to them. So that night, after dinner, Manuel and Jason went to their tent. Later, Jason's dad and the *family* dog, Baxter, went into a tent next to Jason and Manuel.

他们把收音机带到帐篷里，在那里听音乐。

曼纽尔和贾森在帐篷里读书，把最喜欢的玩具带到帐篷里，他们把朋友带到帐篷里，所有的朋友把各自的宠物也带到这里。

他们喜欢待在帐篷里，胜过所有其他的地方，只有回房间里吃饭和睡觉时他们才会离开帐篷。早早地吃完早饭，他们就会回到帐篷。

有一天，他们问父母是否允许他们睡在帐篷里。曼纽尔的父母和贾森的父母都表示同意，但必须让贾森爸爸睡在他们隔壁的帐篷里。所以那天晚上吃过晚饭后，曼纽尔和贾森一起先来到了帐篷，后来贾森的爸爸和家里的狗巴克斯特来到了隔壁的帐篷。

---

favorite adj. 最喜爱的　　　　　　　　breakfast n. 早餐
family adj. 家庭的

GROWING PAINS IV

Soon Manuel and Jason fell fast asleep. And soon Jason's dad and Baxter were fast asleep, too.

Suddenly, there was a loud noise, and it woke Jason up. He reached over and shook Manuel.

"Did you hear that?" he *whispered* loudly.

"No, I didn't hear a thing," said Manuel. "Now, go back to sleep and stop *bothering* me."

Manuel and Jason went back to sleep. Once again, there was a loud noise. And once again, it woke Jason up. Jason jumped up and *frantically* shook Manuel.

"Wake up," he said. "I heard it again. Something is out there."

"I didn't hear anything," said Manuel. "You must be dreaming. I have an *important* baseball game tomorrow morning, and I need

---

曼纽尔和贾森很快就睡着了，接着贾森的爸爸和巴克斯特也睡着了。
突然，出现了一声巨响，把贾森吵醒了，他伸手去摇曼纽尔。
"你听到这个声音了吗？"他压低嗓音，但还是可以听得很清晰。
"没有，我什么都没听到，"曼纽尔说，"好吧，去睡吧，不要烦我了。"
曼纽尔和贾森又睡了，接着又有响声，又把贾森吵醒了，贾森跳了起来，疯了一样地摇着曼纽尔。
"快醒醒！"他说，"我又听到响声了，那里有什么东西？"
"我什么都没听到，"曼纽尔说，"你一定是在做梦吧，明早我还有一场重要的垒球比赛呢。我需要好好地休息，快去睡吧，不要再叫醒我

---

whisper *v.* 小声说
frantically *adv.* 狂乱地；疯狂地

bother *v.* 打扰
important *adj.* 重要的

◆ NOISE IN THE NIGHT

my rest. Go back to sleep and don't wake me up again."

Once again, they fell asleep, but the next time the noise was so loud it woke up both boys. "What was that?" asked Manuel.

"It's the noise I heard before," said Jason.

"Something is *outside* our tent," said Jason. "Get the *flashlight*."

They slowly *unzipped* the tent and looked outside.

They shined a light all around. They shined the light into the woods, and they shined the light up into the trees.

But after looking all around, they saw nothing that could make such a loud noise. So they zipped up the tent and crawled back into their sleeping bags.

了。"

他们又一次睡了，但下一次的声音更大，这回把两个孩子都吵醒了。"那是什么？"曼纽尔问道。

"这就是我刚才听到的声音，"贾森说。

"帐篷外面有什么东西，"贾森说。"去拿手电筒。"

他们慢慢地把帐篷打开，向外望去。

他们四处照了照，照到了旁边的树林，接着又照到了树上。

照完了周围的一切后，他们没有看到什么能发出巨响的东西，这回他们把帐篷关好，钻到了各自的睡袋中。

---

outside *prep.* 在……外面　　　　　　　　flashlight *n.* 手电筒
unzip *v.* 拉开（拉链）

GROWING PAINS IV

◆ NOISE IN THE NIGHT

Then, out of the still of the dark night, they heard the noise again. "Oh, no," said Jason. "Whatever it is, the noise is coming from my dad's tent. Come on. Let's check it out. We have to *save* him."

Both boys *grabbed* baseball bats and quietly stepped toward the tent. They carefully opened the tent where Jason's dad was sound asleep.

And there, inside the tent, they found the *awfully* loud noise. "Dad and Baxter sure do *snore* loudly," said Jason.

这时，从静静的黑夜中，又一次传来了声音。"噢，不要这样，"贾森说，"不管那是什么声音，一定是从爸爸的帐篷里传来的，赶快，我们去看一下，我们必须救他。"

两个孩子抓起垒球棒，轻轻地向帐篷走去。他们小心翼翼地打开帐篷，贾森的爸爸正在里面大睡。

进到帐篷里，他们找到了这巨大声音的来源。"爸爸和巴克斯特的鼾声太大了。"贾森说。

---

save *v.* 拯救
awfully *adv.* 十分；非常

grab *v.* 抓住
snore *n.* 打鼾

GROWING PAINS IV

2

Sammy Stuffit

When Sammy Was Young

What is it about *stuff*? It seems no one can get enough of it. We want bigger stuff, and we want faster stuff. And we want *fancier* stuff. We just seem to want more and more stuff.

There wasn't anyone who liked stuff more than Sammy Stuffit. He began *collecting* stuff when he was five. And he never *quit* collecting it. He just kept getting more stuff, and he kept stashing it away.

萨米——东西控

萨米年轻的时候

东西是怎么回事呢?看起来谁的东西都不够用,我都想让东西更大一些,我们想让东西更快一起,我想让东西更精美一些。我们想要越来越多的东西。

对于东西的需求,几乎没有人能超过东西控小萨米的了,他在5岁时就开始收集东西,而且他从来没有停下来,他不停地收集东西,而且他一直把它们藏起来。

---

stuff *n.* 东西;物品
collect *v.* 收集

fancy *adj.* 精美的
quit *v.* 停止;放弃

◆ SAMMY STUFFIT

GROWING PAINS IV

When Sammy got stuff, he stuffed it somewhere. The more he got, the more he stuffed. He didn't use it. Rather, he just stuffed it. He stuffed it here, he stuffed it there, and he stuffed it everywhere.

When Sammy was five, he stuffed stuff in his *dresser*. He stuffed rocks in his sock drawer. He stuffed baseball cards, *stamps*, and bottle caps in his pants drawer. He stuffed toy cars and *trucks* in drawers. Soon his dresser was so stuffed he had no room for more stuff.

When Sammy turned six, he stuffed stuff in his *closet*. He stuffed stuff under his bed, and he stuffed stuff in the corners of his room. Soon his room became so stuffed with stuff that there was no room for Sammy.

萨米弄到东西时，他会把它们放在某些地方，收集得越多，堆得也越多，但他不会用这些东西，而只是堆起来，这里一堆，那里一堆，堆得到处都是。

萨米5岁时，他把东西塞到他的衣橱中，把小石头塞到他的袜子抽屉中，把垒球卡、邮票、瓶盖放在他的裤子抽屉中，把他的玩具汽车、卡车也放在抽屉中。很快他的衣橱装得满满的，没有地方放别的东西了。

萨米6岁时，他把东西放在他的贮藏柜中，他把东西放在他的床下，放在房间的角落里，很快他的房间也满了，以至于没有他自己的空间了。

---

dresser *n.* 橱柜　　　　　　　　　　　stamp *n.* 邮票
truck *n.* 卡车　　　　　　　　　　　　closet *n.* 壁橱

◆ SAMMY STUFFIT

Sammy Gets Older

As Sammy grew older, he just got more and more stuff. He stuffed the *attic*, the basement, and the garage with stuff. Stuff was everywhere in and around Sammy's house.

Sammy had every game ever made. He didn't have just one of each game. Instead, he had many of each. He had 16 televisions, 24 radios, 9 *stereos*, and 32 bicycles.

He had thousands of books and CDs, and he had computer hardware and *software*. It seemed there was nothing Sammy didn't have. He had more stuff than anyone else on the *planet*.

Years passed. Sammy got even older, and so did much of his stuff. But that didn't stop Sammy from collecting more stuff. And he

---

萨米长大了

随着萨米年龄的增长，他收集的东西越来越多，他把阁楼装满了，地下室装满了，汽车间装满了。萨米的房间里和房子周围都是东西。

萨米拥有人类制造的所有玩具，每一种玩具他不只是有一个，而是有很多，他有16台电视，24部收音机，9个立体音响，32辆自行车。

他有几千本书和CD，他有计算机硬件和软件。好像萨米什么东西都有，他是这个星球上东西最多的人。

很多年过去了，萨米年龄更大了，他的东西也更加多了起来，但这并没有让他放弃收集东西，他从不扔东西，他还要把新收集来的东西与以前

---

attic *n.* 阁楼
software *n.* 软件

stereo *n.* 立体音响
planet *n.* 行星

GROWING PAINS IV

never threw anything away. He just got newer stuff to stuff away with his older stuff.

Every time Sammy *filled* one place *with* stuff, he would buy another place to put more stuff. He bought garages and barns. He bought *warehouses* and boxcars, and he bought barges and boats. And he stuffed them all with more stuff.

When someone asked to borrow some of Sammy's stuff, Sammy refused. He said, "It is my stuff, and I want to keep it safe."

"*Besides*, if I let someone use my stuff, they might not bring it back. It is my stuff and I am going to keep it for myself."

Sammy Begins to *Wonder*

One day, one of Sammy's friends asked, "Sammy, what do you do with all your stuff?"

收集的东西放在一起。

  每一次萨米找到一个地方放东西，他都要再买一个地方放更多的东西，他买车库和谷仓，他买仓库和篷车，他买驳船和船，他要塞更多的东西。

  如果有人向萨米借一些东西，他是不会同意的，他说，"这是我的东西，我要确保它们的安全。"

  "而且，如果我同意让别人用我的东西，他们很可能不会还给我，这是我的东西，我要给自己留着。"

  萨米开始疑惑

  有一天，萨米的一个朋友问，"萨米，你要这么多东西有什么用呢？"

---

fill ... with 用……装满   warehouse *n.* 仓库
besides *prep.* 而且   wonder *v.* 疑惑

◆ SAMMY STUFFIT

Sammy *paused* and thought about it. He thought and thought. Then he scratched his head and he thought some more.

"So, Sammy, what is it you do with all your stuff?" Sammy's friend asked again.

After thinking for what seemed a long, long time, Sammy *finally* answered. "Nothing," Sammy said. "I do *absolutely* nothing with my stuff."

"Then why do you have so much of it?" Sammy's friend asked.

"Because," said Sammy.

"Because why?" pressed his friend.

Sammy didn't know how to answer. So he just *blurted* out, "Because it makes me happy."

萨米停了下来，开始想这件事情，他想呀想，然后他搔了搔头皮，他要多想一下。

"那么，萨米，你想用这些东西干什么呢？"萨米的朋友再一次问他。

萨米想了好像是很长很长的时间，然后回答说，"没有什么用，"萨米说，"这些东西我什么用都没有。"

"那么你为什么有这么多呢？"萨米的朋友问他。

"因为，"萨米说。

"因为什么呢？"他的朋友催促他说。

萨米不知道怎样回答，所以他只是含糊地说，"因为这会让我很高兴。"

---

pause v. 停顿；暂停
absolutely adv. 完全地

finally adv. 最终；终于
blurt v. 未加思索脱口而出

GROWING PAINS IV

"Well, you sure don't seem all that happy," *replied* Sammy's friend. "Besides, how can something you do absolutely nothing with make you happy?"

"Wouldn't all that stuff you have stuffed away make someone who doesn't have much stuff happier than it makes you?"

Sammy didn't know how to *respond* to his friend. He became very *frustrated*. So he just stomped off. But what his friend said made him think about all his stuff. He began to think that maybe there was truth to what his friend had said.

Sammy Changes

He thought about how his stuff just sat in drawers, closets, barns, warehouses, and boxcars. He began to *realize* that he never used it. And he suddenly came to realize it was just stuff.

"好吧，你并不是非常高兴，"萨米的朋友回答说。"而且，一样与你毫无关系的东西怎能让你高兴呢？"

"你所收集的东西能不能让没有这些东西的人比你更快乐一些呢？"

萨米不知道怎样回答他的朋友，他有些受挫，于是他一跺脚就走开了。但是朋友的话让他开始思考自己的东西，他开始想，也许朋友的话有一定的道理。

萨米开始改变

他开始想他抽屉、储藏柜、粮仓、仓库和篷车里存放的东西，他开始意识到他永远都不会用它，他突然意识到这些东西只是东西。

---

reply *v.* 回答
frustrated *adj.* 受挫的；沮丧的

respond *v.* 回答
realize *v.* 意识到

◆ SAMMY STUFFIT

GROWING PAINS IV

So after thinking more and more about his stuff, Sammy *made a decision*. He decided that having so much stuff stuffed away was silly. He thought it made him *selfish*. And he suddenly realized that it didn't really make him happy.

So Sammy gave a little of his stuff to someone who had very little stuff. He saw that the stuff made the person happy, and that made Sammy feel good. So he gave more stuff away, and that made him feel even better.

To Sammy's *surprise*, giving his stuff to others made him happier than having the stuff for himself. Before long, Sammy had given most of his stuff away. He soon became known as Happy Sammy instead of Sammy Stuffit.

所以，萨米越来越多地想这些东西了，他做出了一个决定，他认为把这些东西都堆在这里是一种愚蠢的行为，他认为这会让他很自私，突然他意识到，这并不能使他高兴。

所以，萨米把自己东西的一小部分送给了几乎没有东西的人，他看到这些东西让这个人很高兴，这也让萨米很开心。所以他把更多的东西送给别人，这让他感觉更好。

令萨米惊讶的是，把东西给别人比把东西留给自己更让他高兴，不久，他几乎把自己所有的东西都送出去了，他很快变成了快乐萨米，而不再是东西控萨米了。

---

make a decision 作决定   selfish *adj.* 自私的
surprise *n.* 惊讶

3

♦ THE FOOTPRINT

The Footprint

A Dull Day

It was Saturday morning, and Angie and Jared were *already* bored. Their mother had gone to work, their father was busy cleaning the house, and their elder sister, Sara, was getting ready for a diving trip to Mexico.

"Where's my *snorkel*?" Sara *shouted*. "Where's my *mask*?"

脚印

无聊的一天

这是周六的上午,安吉和贾里德已经开始无聊了,他们的妈妈去上班了,爸爸忙着清理房间,他们的姐姐,萨拉正在准备开车到墨西哥旅行。

"我的水下呼吸管哪去了?"萨拉大声地说,"我的面罩哪去了?"

---

already *adv.* 已经
shout *v.* 叫喊;大叫

snorkel *n.* 水下呼吸管
mask *n.* 面罩

GROWING PAINS IV

Jared *shrugged* and Angie sighed. "Sara gets all the fun," Jared said. "We never get to go anywhere."

Then their little brother, Benjamin, came stomping in from the kitchen, trailing his blanket behind him. "YARGH!!" he yelled. "I'm a *MONSTER*! Act scared!"

But Angie and Jared were tired of acting scared for Benjamin. He was always playing monster.

"Come on, Jared," said Angie. "Let's get out of here before Dad makes us *baby-sit*."

The Footprint

They decided to go exploring by the *creek* that ran behind their

---

贾里德耸了耸肩，安吉叹了一口气，"萨拉都是有趣儿的事儿，"贾里德说，"我们哪里都没有去过。"

这时，他们的弟弟，本杰明从厨房重重地走了进来，把家里的毯子拖在身后，"好呀！"他叫喊着，"我是妖怪！行为吓人！"

但是安吉和贾里德对本杰明的吓人行为感到无聊，他总是装成妖怪。

"来呀，贾里德，"安吉说，"在爸爸还没有安排我们照看孩子之前，我们离开这里。"

脚印

他们决定到小溪边探险，小溪就在他们公寓的后面。他们走在小溪的

---

shrug v. 耸肩
baby-sit v. 照看孩子

monster n. 怪物
creek n. 小溪

◆ THE FOOTPRINT

GROWING PAINS IV

apartment building. As they walked along the bank, Jared saw a strange imprint in the *mud*. "Hey, Angie, look at this!"

They both stared at the print, shaped somewhat like a narrow fan.

"Something with *webbed* toes made this," Angie said. "That must mean it lives in the water."

"It's way too big to be a duck," said Jared. "And look, here's a mark that looks like its tail is dragging in the mud."

"Maybe it's a *completely* new kind of animal," Angie said.

"Or maybe it's a fossil—a *dinosaur* print!" Jared exclaimed.

Jared picked up a stick and poked at the dried mud. The stick

---

岸上，贾里德看到泥土中有一个奇怪的印迹。"喂，安吉，看看这个！"

他们两个看着这个印迹，形状有些像一把窄窄的扇子。

"一种有蹼的东西才能有这样的印迹，"安吉说，"也就是说这种东西一定生活在水中。"

"这种东西在某种程度上比鸭子大得多，"贾里德说。"而且，这里还有一个印迹，像是在泥土上拖着尾巴留下的。"

"说不定是一种全新种类的动物呢，"安吉说。

"或者它可能是化石呢———只恐龙的印迹！"贾里德大叫着。

贾里德拾起一根小棍，捅了一下这块干泥巴。小棍断了。"看看，这

---

mud *n.* 泥
completely *adv.* 完全地

webbed *adj.* 有蹼的
dinosaur *n.* 恐龙

◆ THE FOOTPRINT

broke. "See, this mud is hard. It's *petrified*!"

Angie looked doubtful. "It's just dry because it hasn't rained for weeks."

"You think some living *creature* made this?" Jared asked. "That's pretty scary. *Suppose* it comes after us?"

"Well," said Angie, "we'd better *investigate*!"

Is It a Dinosaur?

Angie and Jared ran home and came back with a notebook, pencil, and tape measure. Jared measured the length and width of the footprint, while Angie drew a sketch of it and the tail marks behind it.

块泥已经硬了,已经石化了!"

安吉表现出怀疑,"只是干了,因为好多天没有下雨了。"

"你认为是现存的生物留下来的这些印迹?"贾里德问,"这可有些吓人,说不定是追我们的呢?"

"好吧,"安吉说,"我们最好调查一下!"

是恐龙吗?

安吉和贾里德跑回家,回来时带着笔记本、铅笔和卷尺。贾里德量出了脚印的长度和宽度,安吉画了它的素描和后面尾巴留下的形态。

---

petrified *adj.* 石化的
suppose *v.* 推断;设想

creature *n.* 生物
investigate *v.* 调查

GROWING PAINS IV

"We should also make a map of where the creek is and where we found the print," she said. "Then we'll go to the library."

But when they stepped into the city library with their map and drawing, they felt *overwhelmed*. So many shelves of books, all the way to the ceiling—they did not know where to begin.

"Can I help you?" asked a *librarian*.

Jared *nudged* Angie, and she stepped forward to *explain* what they were looking for. "My brother thinks this is a dinosaur print," she ended by saying, "but I think it might be some kind of water bird."

"I believe some dinosaur footprints were recently discovered in Utah," said the librarian. "We'll see if they're anything like your print."

"我们还应该画一张小溪的位置图，标上我们是在哪里发现的印迹，"她说，"然后我们去图书馆。"

但是在他们带着画的图来到市图书馆时，他们却不知所措了，这里有很多书，都摆到天花板那么高——他们不知道从哪里开始。

"我能帮助你们吗？"一位图书馆管理员问他们。

贾里德捅了一下安吉，她向前一步说明他们想要的东西，"我哥哥认为这是恐龙的脚印，"她最后说，"但是我认为这只是某种水禽。"

"我想最近在犹他州发现了某些恐龙的脚印，"图书馆管理员说，"我们看看这些是不是像你们的脚印。"

---

overwhelm *v.* 使不知所措
nudge *v.* 轻推；轻碰

librarian *n.* 图书馆管理员
explain *v.* 解释

◆ THE FOOTPRINT

The librarian led them to a computer and *typed* in a website address. "Here's the site," she said. "See if this helps; then come to me if you have any more questions."

Jared and Angie crowded up to the computer screen. They read about dinosaur prints that were found when a top layer of earth was *turned over*.

"But our print was right there on the *surface*," said Jared. "That means it can't be a *fossil*, after all. Maybe it's a bird, like you thought."

"Maybe," Angie agreed.

Is It a Bird?

They went back to the librarian.

图书馆管理员把他们带到计算机前，输入一个网址。"这就是网址，"她说，"看看对你们有没有帮助，如果你们有别的问题可以再来找我。"

贾里德和安吉挤到计算机的屏幕前，他们读了有关人类发现的恐龙的脚印，这些脚印都是在翻土地的时候被发现的。

"但是我们找到的脚印都是在表层的，"贾里德说，"所以，这就说明这不可能是化石，也可能是一种鸟类的，与你想的相同。"

"很有可能，"安吉表示同意。

这是鸟吗？

他们回去找图书馆管理员。

---

type *v.* 用打字机打（字）   turn over 翻转
surface *n.* 表面；表层   fossil *n.* 化石

GROWING PAINS IV

"Where can we find out about birds?" Angie asked. The librarian pointed to an old man sitting at a table, *surrounded* by books.

"You're in luck," she whispered. "That's *Professor* Featherwhite; he's an expert on water birds. I'm sure he'll be interested in your footprint. I'll *introduce* you."

The professor looked closely at Angie's drawing and made a clucking noise.

"Hmm, hmm. Very unusual. I don't know of any birds in this area that could have made that print. It's quite large, but perhaps a *migratory* bird from some faraway place..."

"Got blown off course?" asked Jared, finishing the professor's sentence.

"我们在哪里能搞清楚这些鸟呢?"安吉问,图书馆管理员指着一个坐在桌子前的老头儿,他的身边都是书。

"你们今天的运气很好,"她小声说,"那是菲泽怀特教授,他是水禽专家,我想他对你们的脚印一定会非常感兴趣,我把你们介绍给他。"

教授仔细地看了安吉的图,发出咯咯的笑声。

"嗯,很特别,我知道这里的鸟类没有这样的脚印,这脚印很大,也可能是从很远的地方迁徙过来的鸟……"

"飞错航线了?"贾里德问,接着说教授没说完的话。

---

surround *v.* 包围
introduce *v.* 介绍

professor *n.* 教授
migratory *adj.* 迁徙的

◆ THE FOOTPRINT

"Well, yes, *possibly*," said the professor. "Here's a book that might help you. Good luck!"

It was a large book, full of pictures, and so heavy that Angie and Jared had to take turns carrying it home. They took the book *straight* to Angie's room and pored over page after page of birds with webbed feet. But nothing looked right.

"I don't think we'll find any bird big enough to leave a print like that," said Jared. "And besides, what about the tail marks?"

"It could be a bird with a long tail, like a *peacock*," said Angie.

"Peacocks aren't water birds!" cried Jared.

"Oh, well, maybe we've discovered the new water-peacock," Angie said.

"嗯，是的，非常有可能，"教授说。"这里有一本书，可能对你们有用，祝你们好运！"

这是本很大的书，里面全都是图片。这本书太重了，所以安吉和贾里德需要轮流拿着它回家。他们把书直接拿到安吉的房间，研读每一页上有蹼的鸟，但没有一个能对上的。

"我看咱们找到的鸟都没有大到留下这样的脚印，"贾里德说，"而且，还有尾巴的印迹呢？"

"可能是一种有长尾巴的鸟，像孔雀。"安吉说。

"孔雀不是水禽！"贾里德大声说。

"嗯，嗯，说不定我们发现了一种新的水孔雀呢，"安吉说。

---

possibly *adv.* 可能地；或许　　　　straight *adv.* 直接地；径直地
peacock *n.* 孔雀

GROWING PAINS IV

◆ THE FOOTPRINT

Suddenly there was a banging on the door.

"Let me in! Let me in!"

It was Benjamin.

Jared Solves the Mystery

Angie opened the door, and Benjamin *tumbled* in, *clutching* something under his shirt. They could hear Sara running down the hallway outside. "Come back here!" she yelled. "Give me my fin!"

"Benjamin," Angie said *sternly*, "Are you stealing Sara's swim *fins* again?"

Jared closed the door. "Angie—that's it!"

"What?"

"Sara's fin made our footprint! Give it to me, Ben!"

突然传来撞击门的声音。
"让我进来，让我进来！"
这是本杰明的声音。
贾里德找到了秘密的答案
安吉打开了门，本杰明跌跌撞撞地走了进来，他衣服下面掖着什么东西。他们还能听到萨拉在外面的走廊里奔跑的声音，"给我回来！"她大叫着，"把我的脚蹼还给我！"
"本杰明，"安吉严肃地说，"你是不是又偷了萨拉的脚蹼了？"
贾里德关上了门，"安吉——就是它！"
"什么？"
"萨拉的脚蹼留下的脚印，把它给我，本！"

---

tumble *v.* 摔倒；跌倒　　　　　　　　clutch *v.* 紧握；紧抓
sternly *adv.* 严肃地　　　　　　　　　fin *n.* 鳍状物

GROWING PAINS IV

"Oh, no—of course!" Angie said, *slapping* her forehead, while Benjamin pulled the fin out from under his shirt.

"Ben, were you down by the creek awhile ago?" Jared asked.

"Nooooo." Ben said *innocently*. "Well, a long time ago."

Meanwhile Angie measured the fin and compared it to their drawing and notes. "You're right, Jared—it's an almost *perfect* fit." Then she noticed the blanket tucked into Benjamin's shorts. "The tail marks must have been his blanket!"

Benjamin *grinned* up at them. "You mean you found my monster print?"

"噢，不——当然！"安吉说，拍着自己的脑门，这时本杰明从衣服下面拖出了这个脚蹼。

"本，你是不是以前去过小溪？"贾里德问。

"没——有，"本无辜地说，"好吧，那是很早以前的事儿了。"

这时，安吉也在测量这个脚蹼，把它与画和记录作了对比，"你是对的，贾里德——几乎完全相配，"然后她注意到塞在本杰明短裤中的毯子，"那个尾巴印迹就是他的毯子！"

本杰明朝他们笑了一下，"你们是说发现了我这个妖怪的脚印了？"

---

slap *v.* 拍
perfect *adj.* 完美的

innocently *adv.* 无辜地；故作天真地
grin *v.* 露齿而笑

◆ THE FOOTPRINT

Angie and Jared looked at each other and *laughed*.

"First we thought it was a dinosaur," said Jared.

"Then we thought it was a bird," said Angie. "But now we know it was the scariest monster in the whole world!" And she gave Benjamin a hug.

安吉和贾里德看了看彼此,都笑了起来。

"开始时我们认为是恐龙,"贾里德说。

"后来,我们认为是鸟,"安吉说,"但现在我们知道,这是世界上最吓人的妖怪!"说着,她给了本杰明一个大大的拥抱。

---

laugh *v.* 大笑

GROWING PAINS IV

4

Walking in Rome Footsteps

Bound for Rome

Andria and Rosa live in New York City with their parents. They know that their great grandparents and earlier *ancestors* lived in Italy. The girls' parents take them on a trip to Rome, Italy, to learn about their family's past.

After landing at the *airport* in Rome, they check into their hotel and then take a city tour. First, they see where their ancestors lived.

走入罗马的台阶

向罗马进军

安德丽亚和罗莎与父母住在纽约城，他们知道他们的太祖父母以及更早的祖先们住在意大利。女孩子的父母带着她们到意大利罗马旅行，了解她们家族的历史。

在罗马机场落地后，他们在一个旅馆登记入住，然后就在城里参观。首先，他们看了祖先居住的地方，然后两个小姑娘知道有的地方是在2600年以前修建的。在她们看到的这些古老的废墟中有角斗场、罗马商

---

ancestor n. 祖先   airport n. 机场

◆ WALKING IN ROME FOOTSTEPS

GROWING PAINS IV

Then the girls learn about some of the places built over 2,600 years ago. Among the *ancient* ruins they see are those of the Colosseum, the Roman Forum, and the Teatro (tay-AH-trow) Marcello.

After exploring more of Rome's historic streets, the family stops in the Piazza (pea-AHtsa) Navona for lunch. Shops and cafes line the outside of its *oval* shape. In the center, artists gather to sell their paintings near the *fountains*.

In the piazza, the family eats mozzarella (motsuh-REL-uh) and tomato panini (pa-NEE-nee), then they watch the costumed performers—who are standing as still as statues. When someone drops a coin in the bucket in front of the performers, they move like a mechanical wind-up doll. Then stop and stand totally still once again.

业广场和罗马马切罗剧场。

　　对罗马的历史性的街道有了进一步了解后，全家人在纳沃那广场停了下来吃午饭。纳沃那广场为椭圆形，外侧是商店、咖啡店。在中心，艺术家聚集到喷泉这里出售他们的绘画。

　　在广场，全家人吃莫泽雷勒干酪和保尼蒂土豆，然后他们看了穿着戏装的表演者，他们站在那里如同雕像一样不动。如果有人往这些人面前的小桶里丢一个硬币的话，他们就会像一个上了弦的机器娃娃一样动一下，然后就停下来，又站在那里一动不动。

---

ancient *adj.* 古老的　　　　　　　　　　　　oval *adj.* 椭圆形的
fountain *n.* 喷泉

◆ WALKING IN ROME FOOTSTEPS

Dance to the Past

The family buys gelato (je-LAH-toe) and walks among the art booths. The girls hear *tinkling* bells and notice a group of women dancing in *swirling* skirts. Then one of the dancers smiles strangely, right at the sisters. She draws Andria and Rosa into the dance. When the woman says something to them in her native tongue, the girls flash worried looks at their parents. But their parents only smile at them and clap with the music.

As the *performers* keep whirling the girls around, everything around them blurs. Andria and Rosa feel *dizzy*, so they sit down by a fountain and search the crowd for their parents' faces. But something's wrong—the crowd is now dressed in ancient-looking

---

参加过去的跳舞

全家人买了冰激凌，在这些货摊中间步行，女孩们听着响铃声，发现有一群女人正穿着大裙子跳舞。其中有一个舞者笑得很奇怪，正对着这两个姐妹笑。她把安德丽亚和罗莎拉进来跳舞。这个女人用当地的话对她们说话，两个女孩子向父母表现出紧张的神情，但是父母只是冲他们笑了一下，和着音乐拍手。

表演者与孩子们一直转着，周围的一切就变得模糊不清了。安德丽亚和罗莎觉得有些头晕，所以她们坐在喷泉旁边，在人群中找父母的脸。但是出了一点状况，现在这群人穿上了古代人的衣服，街道上没有汽车，只

---

tinkle　*v.*　发叮当声　　　　　　　　　swirl　*v.*　旋动；打旋
performer　*n.*　表演者　　　　　　　　dizzy　*adj.*　头晕目眩的

GROWING PAINS IV

clothes. Instead of cars, horses and *chariots* have filled the streets. The girls look at each other with wide eyes, not understanding what has happened.

Andria feels a gentle touch on her shoulder. The *gypsy* woman who included them in the dance is next to her, talking. But now Andria can understand her words. The dancer tells the girls, "You have been taken back in time to learn how Rome was built—layer upon layer, new upon old. To return to your own time, you must *discover* three places where the new is built on or around the old. Each time you do, you will get a surprise."

The girls begin by taking a chariot ride to the Colosseum. But it looks different. The worn and broken red *brick* walls they saw on the

---

有马和战车。两个女孩子相互看了一下，眼睛睁得大大的，不知道发生了什么事情。

安德丽亚感到肩上被人轻轻地拍了一下，一个吉卜赛女人，就是刚才接她们跳舞的那个人，就在她的旁边，正在说话。但是安德丽亚能听懂她说的话了。这个舞者告诉两个女孩子，"你们被带回到过去的时代了，了解一下罗马是怎样建成的，是一层层建的，新的建在旧的上面。要想回到你们自己的时代，你们必须找到三个在旧的上面或周围新建的地方，每次完成以后，你们都有一个惊喜。"

女孩子先是乘战车到达角斗场，但它很不同。她们在城市观光时见到

---

chariot　*n.*　双轮马车；战车
discover　*v.*　发现

gypsy　*n.*　吉卜赛人
brick　*n.*　砖；砖块

◆ WALKING IN ROME FOOTSTEPS

city tour have *disappeared*. And its tall, *circular* shape is whole again. It looks new—and now stands covered with gleaming white marble. The *awnings* at the top are unrolled, giving shade to the thousands of *spectators* inside. Andria and Rosa hear the crowd roar as the Roman citizens watch the games.

Rosa remembers hearing their family's tour guide explain that marble once covered the walls, steps, and seats of the Colosseum. And that, when St. Peter's Basilica was built in Vatican City, on the other side of Rome, some of the Colosseum's marble was used to cover the floors. Suddenly Rosa feels something heavy in her pocket—and excitedly pulls out a gold coin to show Andria. Big grins spread across their faces. They are on the right track!

的破烂的红砖墙不见了。它现在是高大、环行的一个整体，看起来很新，外面覆盖着闪光的白色大理石。上面的雨篷还没有打开，为里面无数的观众遮挡阳光。安德丽亚和罗莎听到人们正呼喊着，这些罗马市民正在看比赛。

罗莎记得她家的导游介绍过，角斗场的墙、台阶和座位的表面都是大理石的，圣彼得天主教堂是在梵蒂冈城建的，在罗马的另一侧，角斗场的一些大理石用来铺在地面上。突然罗莎感到衣袋里有很重的东西，让她兴奋的是，她从衣袋里取出的是一枚金币，她拿给安德丽亚看。她们的脸上出现了笑容，她们的路线是正确的。

disappear *v.* 消失　　　　　　　　　　　circular *adj.* 圆形的
awning *n.* 雨篷；遮阳篷　　　　　　　　spectator *n.* 观众

GROWING PAINS IV

From the Colosseum, they follow the *rough* stone street up the hill to the Roman Forum. Andria circles the Arch of Titus, built in about AD 84, looking for the road made of large stones that they had walked on the day before. They saw the road with their parents. But now—it isn't there.

Andria realizes why. When this arch was built people couldn't see the street, either—it was covered by *centuries* of dirt! Augustus Caesar had built the ancient street in 6 BC. Almost a hundred years later, Titus built the *arch* on top of the dirt. Even back then, the Romans were building on and around their past. Andria feels a weight in her pocket. She pulls out a gold coin and waves it in *triumph*!

离开了角斗场，她们沿着粗石铺的街道向山坡走去，这就是罗马商业广场。提图斯凯旋门建于公元84年，安德丽亚绕提图斯凯旋门走着，想找到前一天走过的用大石铺成的路。他们和父母一起看到过这条路，但这条路不见了。

安德丽亚明白了原因，在修这个凯旋门时，人们是看不到街道的，上面覆盖着几个世纪以来形成的泥土！奥古斯塔斯·恺撒在公元前6年修建了这条街道。几乎正好一百年以后，提图斯在这些泥土上修建了这个凯旋门。就是在当时，罗马人也是在过去的建筑物上面或周围修东西。安德丽亚感觉到衣袋一沉，她取出一枚金币，高兴地挥舞着！

---

rough *adj.* 粗糙不平的
arch *n.* 拱门
century *n.* 世纪；一百年
triumph *n.* 狂喜；极大的满足

◆ WALKING IN ROME FOOTSTEPS

GROWING PAINS IV

The girls walk through the Roman Forum and up Capitoline Hill. On their left, they see the ancient *pillars* and arches of Teatro Marcello. They both remember their guide telling them that new condominiums have been built above the old arches of the teatro. And they see that the church next door used pillars of an ancient building to make part of its outside wall. A third gold coin rolls in the street toward them!

Pockets Full of Coins

Andria and Rosa found their three *clues*! *Immediately*, the past melts away, and once again they hear the honking of car horns. It's today again—and the dancer is beside them. She leads them to the Pantheon. Andria points to the 15-foot *slope* next to the ancient

---

两个女孩穿过罗马商业广场，登上卡匹托尔山。在她们的左侧，她们看到了古代的柱子和罗马马切罗剧场拱门。她们两个都记着导游告诉他们，这个新的公寓套房是在一个旧凯旋门剧场上建起来的。她们还看到旁边的教堂采用了古建筑的柱子作为它的外墙。第三枚金币从街上向她们滚了过来。

衣袋里装满了硬币

安德丽亚和罗莎找到了三个线索，很快过去的一切就消失了，她们又一次听到了汽车的喇叭声。这又是现实世界了，舞者又出现在她们身边，

---

pillar *n.* 柱子
immediately *adv.* 立即；马上

clue *n.* 线索
slope *n.* 斜坡

◆ WALKING IN ROME FOOTSTEPS

temple and says "See, the street *level* of today is much higher than the street used to be."

The girls now know that without the past, the new would have nothing to stand on. In many ways, the new *depends on* the old. After *nodding* to each other with pride, they see their parents waiting for them with open arms. The girls run to them, waving their coins and shouting, "Let's get more gelato!"

舞者把她们带到罗马万神庙，这个建筑与古庙挨着。安德丽亚指着这个15英尺高的斜坡说，"看呀，今天街道的修建水平比过去的高很多。"

女孩子们现在知道了，如果没有过去，新的建筑是没有地方建立的。在很多方面，新的要依赖于旧的。两个人自豪地冲对方点了点头，这时她们看到父母正张开双臂等着她们。女孩们向父母跑去，挥动着金币喊着，"我们再弄一些冰淇淋！"

---

temple *n.* 庙宇；寺院　　　　　　　　　　level *n.* 水平；等级
depend on　依赖　　　　　　　　　　　　　nod *v.* 点头

Neighborhood Mystery

Strange Cases

I have seen it at the same house, at the same time, every sunday night for the last three months. A group of *individuals*, some of them *slim*, some of them *stout*, most of them male, but some of them female, entering this house across the street from me.

Each of them wears a similar looking *uniform* and carries some kind of case.

街区秘密

奇怪的盒子

我在同一间房子里看到过它,同样的时间,每个周日的晚上,已经有三个月了。有一群人,有的瘦,有的结实,但大都是男人,有一些是女的,从我面对的街过来进了这所房子。

他们都穿着相似的制服,都带着一个盒子。

---

individual *n.* 个人
stout *adj.* 结实的;肥胖的
slim *adj.* 苗条的;纤细的
uniform *n.* 制服

◆ NEIGHBORHOOD MYSTERY

I know they are not carrying *luggage*. Most of the cases are too small for that. One of the cases is huge! Only some are *square* while others have a *weird* curvy shape. At 7:00 P.M., it is hard to see anything clearly—especially if your neighborhood does not have *streetlights*.

Aside from the porch lights and the passing cars, I can't see much of anything in the darkness.

All the people walking into the house seem to be wearing the same dark color, but down along their sides, there is a line of shiny buckles, catching flickers of light from the porch light. I wonder what it all means.

I never saw anything like this while living in Boston; but, I do remember seeing strange reports on television that might help

---

我知道他们拿的不是行李，大多数的盒子太小了，不能装行李。但有一个盒子是非常大的！只有少数盒子是方形的，其他的都是怪怪的弧线形。到了下午七点，这时已经很难看清楚东西了，特别是如果你的邻居没有街灯的时候。

除了弧光灯和路过的汽车以外，在黑暗中我看不到太多的东西。

所有走进房子的人好像都穿着同一种暗色的衣服，但是身体两侧下方，有一排闪亮的扣子，一闪一闪地反射出廊灯灯光，我不知道这是什么意思。

生活在波士顿的我从未见过像这样的东西，但我的确记得在电视上看到过奇怪的报道，这可能会帮助我解释这些东西。首先我不敢告诉学校里

---

luggage *n.* 行李
weird *adj.* 奇怪的

square *adj.* 正方形的
streetlight *n.* 街灯；路灯

41

explain things. At first, I was afraid to tell anyone at school about my neighborhood *mystery* because I was afraid they would think I was acting strange. But then, I got up the *courage* to ask my friend Maria, who lives in my neighborhood, if she knew anything about the strange happenings.

I caught her in the hallway, after school, as she was opening her locker and reaching inside. She pulled out a small case.

I froze.

She turned to look at me and saw my startled face. "What?" she *exclaimed*.

"Haven't you seen a violin case before?"

的其他人关于邻居家的秘密，因为担心他们会认为我的行为特殊，但是当时我鼓起了勇气问我的朋友，玛丽亚，看她知不知道这奇怪的事情，她住得离我不远。

放学后我在走廊里遇到了她，她正在开她的储物柜，把手伸进去取出一个小盒子。

我惊呆了。

她转过身来看着我，看到我很惊讶的表情。"什么事儿？"她大声说。

"你以前没有看过小提琴盒子吗？"

---

explain *v.* 解释　　　　　　　　　mystery *n.* 谜；神秘的事物
courage *n.* 勇气　　　　　　　　　exclaim *v.* 突然呼喊；惊叫

◆ NEIGHBORHOOD MYSTERY

Of course, I had seen one before. After all, I was born in Boston, hometown of the one of the most famous *symphony orchestras* in the world—the Boston Pops. My family heard them play on every Fourth of July. Last year, I counted 30 violins in that orchestra! So, yes, I've seen my share of violin cases.

In fact, my dad rented a violin to see if I would like it, but I really wanted to play the *guitar*. The violin, now that I think of it, came in a case just like Maria's. Maybe I was too busy thinking about the mystery to make the *connection*.

"Did you need something?" she asked.

"Never mind," I said as I walked away confused and deep in thought ...

当然了，我以前见过，不管怎么说，我出生在波士顿，世界最有名的交响乐团故乡之———波士顿流行音乐乐队。我们家每年的7月4日都听他们演奏。去年我数了数乐队中的小提琴，共有30把！所以，是的，我看到过小提琴盒子。

事实上，我爸爸还给我租了一把小提琴，看看我是否喜欢，但我真正喜欢的是弹吉他。小提琴，现在我认为，是放在盒子里的，与玛丽亚的是一样的。可能是我太急于思考这些秘密了，而没有把这些东西联系起来。

"你需要什么东西吗？"她问我。

"不要在意，"我边说边走开了，有些糊涂，我不禁陷入了沉思⋯⋯

---

symphony *n.* 交响乐；交响曲 orchestra *n.* 管弦乐队
guitar *n.* 吉他 connection *n.* 联系

GROWING PAINS IV

Who were those people with the cases? I could not be sure. The only way to know would be to *solve* the mystery myself—like a *detective*.

My Stakeout

On Sunday, I made my plan and gathered up a flashlight, *binoculars*, a whistle, dog biscuits, and my dog. I waited by my window for the sun to go down. When I saw 7:00 on my clock, I knew that my detective work would begin.

I waited until the whole group of people had gone inside because I was afraid of what might happen if anyone saw me. When all was clear, I got my things and my dog and *sneaked* over to the house across the street.

那些带着盒子的人是谁呢？我不确定。弄明白的唯一方法是我自己解开这个谜——像侦探一样。

我的监视

今天是周日，我制订了一个计划，准备好手电筒、一副双筒望远镜、一个口哨、狗饼干，还有我的狗。我在窗边等着太阳落山。我看着钟已经到了下午7点，我知道我的侦探工作就要开始了。

我一直等着这群人进入房子，因为我担心如果有人看到我会怎么样。当一切看清楚后，我带上我的东西和我的狗，溜到了街对面的房子。

solve *v.* 解决（问题）	detective *n.* 侦探
binoculars *n.* 双筒望远镜	sneak *v.* 偷偷地走；潜行

◆ NEIGHBORHOOD MYSTERY

GROWING PAINS IV

It's a good thing that there are big trees and bushes for me to hide behind, I thought.

I went from tree to bush to tree until I got close enough to a window to hear something. I started to hear some talking. Yet, I could not understand the language. Maybe they were talking in code?

Then, there was *laughter*. One loud, deep laugh shook me like a leaf. It sounded like some kind of *eerie* Santa Claus. It must have come from a very big man.

My dog *growled* like he was about to bark so I gave him a biscuit to keep him quiet. Then I heard deep string-plucking sounds that *vibrated* the windows of the house. Some screeching sounds followed.

"这里有大树和灌木可真好,我可以藏在后面。"我想。

我从一棵树到灌木,再到另一棵树,一直到接近窗户能听到什么。我开始听到有人在说话,但是我不能理解他们的语言。或许他们是用密语交谈的?

接着,屋里传来了笑声。一阵很大、低沉的笑声震得我像聋了一样,这声音有些像令人恐惧的圣诞老人的笑声,这笑声一定是来自一个身材高大的男人。

我的狗吠叫起来,好像是要大叫起来,等着我给它一块饼干,让它安静下来。然后我听到低沉的拨弦的声音,这使得房子的窗户也跟着颤动起

---

laughter *n.* 笑声
growl *v.* 低声吼叫

eerie *adj.* 可怕的;怪异的
vibrate *v.* 使颤动

◆ NEIGHBORHOOD MYSTERY

These sounds reminded me of the *violinists* in the Boston Pops just before they performed.

Now it was starting to make sense. They must be *musicians* of some kind; but, with so few of them, they could not be a symphony orchestra. My dad once told me that the Boston Symphony Orchestra has more than 90 musicians. My thoughts were *interrupted* by a sudden sound, like a car horn.

My Discovery

I was sure it came from inside the house even as another car drove up. My dog started to bark like crazy. He jumped out of the bushes and pulled me with him. I *accidentally* turned on my flashlight. It shined on someone right in front of me. It was Maria!

来。接下来是嘶嘶的声音。

在他们演奏之前，这些声音让我想起了波士顿流行乐队中的小提琴手。

现在这些东西有些清楚了。他们可能是某种音乐家，但是他们就这么几个人，不可能是一个交响乐队。我爸爸曾告诉过我，波士顿交响乐团有九十多个音乐家。我的思考被一阵突如其来的声音打断，好像是汽车的喇叭声。

我的发现

我敢保证，这声音是从房子里传出来的，尽管还有一辆车开了过来。我的狗开始叫了起来，像疯了一样。他从灌木后面跳出来，拖着我。我一不小心把手电筒打开了，正好照在了我前面的一个人身上，原来是玛丽亚！

---

violinist *n.* 小提琴手；小提琴演奏家 musician *n.* 音乐家
interrupt *v.* 打断   accidentally *adv.* 偶然地

GROWING PAINS IV

"Alan? What are you doing here?"

"Uh, I, um."

"Did you come to hear the mariachi at my uncle Eduardo's house?"

"Mah-ree-AHchee? What is that?" I asked.

"It is a *Mexican folk* band. Want to come in and listen?" "Mystery solved! Case closed!" I said to myself.

Just then, my dad came out of the garage of our house across the street to take the garbage can out to the *curb*. I yelled out to him asking if he wanted to hear the band of Maria's uncle, too. He smiled and yelled back to us "¡Sí!," which means yes!

Soon, we were inside sitting on the couch as we watched and listened to the mariachi group playing their *instruments*. Three

---

"艾伦？你在这里做什么呢？"

"噢，我，嗯。"

"你是不是来爱德华多叔叔家听mariachi的？"

"Mah-ree-Ahchee?那是什么意思？"我问。

"这是墨西哥的民间乐队，想进来听一听吗？" "谜底揭开了！结案！"我对自己说。

就在这时，我爸爸从街对面家里的车库出来，正在往路边送垃圾，我向他喊着，问他是否也想听玛丽亚叔叔的乐队演奏。他笑着喊道，"¡Sí！"，意思是好的。

很快，我们都坐在沙发上，我们欣赏着这民间乐队演奏各自的乐器，

Mexican *adj.* 墨西哥的   folk *adj.* 民间的
curb *n.* 路缘   instrument *n.* 乐器

◆ NEIGHBORHOOD MYSTERY

members of the group played violins, another three played guitars, and two others played *trumpets*. One of the violinists sang and the others joined in for the chorus. We heard many mariachi songs that night. They sounded *fantastic*.

Mariachi songs are in Spanish. Before that night, there was only one word other than "yes" that I knew in Spanish and that was the word "gracias", which means thank you. That is what I told Maria when she led my father and me into the house.

I learned many new Spanish words that night. The words "violín", "guitarra", and "trompeta" were very easy to *memorize* because they look and sound a lot like the English words "violin", "guitar", and "trumpet". The name of the huge bass guitar, "guitarrón", was

---

这个乐队中有三个小提琴手，另外还有三个吉他手，两个小号手。一位小提琴手主唱，其他人加入进来合唱，那天晚上我们听了很多民间乐队歌曲，听起来真是妙极了。

这些民间乐队歌曲都是西班牙语的，在那一天晚上之前，除了西班牙语"是"这个词，我只知道一个词，"gracias"，意思是"谢谢你"，玛丽亚把我和爸爸带到那所房子里时，我向她说了这个词。

那天晚上我学会了很多新的西班牙语词，"小提琴"、"吉他"和"鼓"这三个词很好记，因为他们听起来和英语的"小提琴"、"吉他"和"鼓"很接近。大低音吉他，"guitarrón"，有一点儿难记。这听起来

---

trumpet n. 小号 　　　　　fantastic adj. 极好的；极妙的
memorize v. 记住

GROWING PAINS IV

◆ NEIGHBORHOOD MYSTERY

a little harder to remember. I think it funny that the smallest guitar had the most difficult name to learn—vihuela (vee-WEH-la). This instrument is smaller than a *regular* guitar but larger than those *tiny* guitars from Hawaii called ukulele (u-keh-LAY-lee).

As it turned out, the mystery led me to discover new things about another culture. I want to learn more. So I hope Dad will let me take guitar lessons at school next year. When I get good enough, I want to learn songs like the one called "Las Mañanitas" ("The Little Mornings"). Then I may buy a *sombrero* and *serenade* for Maria—just like a real mariachi!

很奇怪，最小的吉他有一个最难学会的名字——vihuela。这个乐器比吉他小，但比来自于夏威夷的小型吉他大，即夏威夷四弦吉他。

事实的结果是，秘密引导我发现了另一种文化，我还想多了解一些。所以我希望爸爸同意我明年在学校参加吉他课程。等我学到一定程度时，我也想学一个像"Las Mañanitas"（"小小的早晨"）这样的歌曲。然后我就可以买一个阔边毡帽，去给玛丽亚演奏小夜曲——就像一个真正的民间乐队一般！

---

regular *adj.* 普通的；常见的
sombrero *n.* 男士宽边帽

tiny *adj.* 极小的
serenade *v.* 为……演奏小夜曲

GROWING PAINS IV

6

The Black Stones

The Stones

Tala glanced over her *shoulder* before she picked up the two small, black stones near the river's edge at the base of Apache Leap Mountain. If her brother was watching, he'd want the stones for himself, and she didn't want to give them to him. She had discovered them, and they were hers.

Paco was busy tossing *pebbles* into the river, so Tala *knelt down*

黑石记

石头

塔拉在阿帕奇飞跃山脚下的小河边发现了两颗很小的黑色石头，在把石头捡起来之前，塔拉扭过头去看了一下。如果她哥哥看到了石头，一定会据为己有的，她可不想把石头给哥哥。是她发现了这两块石头，石头就应该是她的。

趁着帕科往河里扔鹅卵石扔得正欢，塔拉跪下去，捡起这两块闪闪发亮的黑石头。石头的颜色就如同无星无月的夜空一样漆黑。当她把石头举

---

shoulder n. 肩膀
kneel down 跪下

pebble n. 鹅卵石

◆ THE BLACK STONES

and picked up the *shimmering* black stones, which were as dark as the blackest *starless* night. When she held them up to the sun, the light glittered through them, changing them to a clear, *translucent* color.

"Let me see!" her brother called.

Tala groaned and clutched the stones tightly in her fist. If she was quick enough, she might be able to hide them from her *annoying* twin.

Tala hugged her knees and listened to her brother's footsteps as he leapt from rock to rock, moving closer and closer.

When he was behind her, she rose and started to walk away.

"Come on!" Paco said. "Show me what's in your hand."

起来对着太阳时，阳光打在石头上，石头闪闪发光，进而变成了清澈的半透明色。

"让我看看！"她的哥哥喊道。

塔拉暗叫不妙，紧紧握住了石头。如果她动作再快点，她就能在帕科来之前把石头藏起来。她真是烦透了这个双胞胎哥哥。

塔拉双手环膝，听着她哥哥大步跃过一块块岩石，脚步声一点点靠近。

帕科刚到她身后，她起身就要走开。

"别走啊！"帕科说，"给我看看你手里的东西。"

---

shimmer *v.* 发微光；闪烁
translucent *adj.* 半透明的；透明般的

starless *adj.* 无星的
annoying *adj.* 令人厌烦的

◆ THE BLACK STONES

Tala knew that if she revealed the stones, her brother would *implore* and *beseech* and beg her to give them to him. She knew that he would keep on begging until she became *furious*, or gave in.

Tala swung around. "These stones are mine!" she shouted. "I found them, and I'm keeping them, no matter what you say!"

"Just show them to me!" Paco shouted back as he grabbed her fist and tried to pry it open.

"MOM!" Tala cried. "MOM! Paco's bothering me again!"

Mrs. Yates sighed and raised herself from the flat rock where she had been sitting for the *peaceful* last half hour. The twins hadn't been fighting, which was unusual for them, but things were back to normal now. They were at it again. If only they could learn to get

---

塔拉知道如果她暴露了这两块石头，她哥哥就会恳求、哀求加乞求地把石头要走。她也知道，只要她不发火，也不让步，帕科就会一直乞求下去。

塔拉转过身来，"这些石头是我的！"她喊道，"是我找到的，就得放在我这，你说什么都没用！"

"我就看一眼！"帕科也不甘示弱地喊道。他说着就过来抓塔拉的手，用足了力气要撬开她的拳头。

"妈！"塔拉大喊道，"妈！帕科又来烦我了！"

耶茨太太叹了口气，从平滑的岩石上站了起来。她在这岩石上坐了半个小时，那对双胞胎十分反常地没有吵架，她觉得那半个小时简直是人间天堂，可是现在这两个孩子又恢复正常了——他们又吵起来

---

implore *v.* 恳求 beseech *v.* 央求；哀求
furious *adj.* 狂怒的；暴怒的 peaceful *adj.* 宁静的；平静的

GROWING PAINS IV

along, she thought as she made her way down to the riverbank. If only they could be good friends.

Mrs. Yates dragged her twins apart and sat them down on either side of her. She *decided* to let them calm down before she said anything. Maybe this time things would be different; maybe one of them would *apologize*—but neither Paco nor Tala said a word.

Tala clutched her stones tightly and thought about how the river had *polished* and smoothed them.

"I was the one who found the stones!" she said when she had *calmed down* a bit. "Paco tried to take them away from me. It's his fault. I didn't do anything."

"Yes, you did!" Paco insisted. "You wouldn't even let me see

了。耶茨太太沿着河岸边走边想，他们要是学会好好地相处该有多好，他们俩要是能成为好朋友该有多好。

耶茨太太把两个孩子拉开，让他们坐在自己身边，一边一个。她什么都没说，想让孩子们自己先冷静冷静。说不定这次事情会有转机，说不定有一个人会主动道歉——可是帕科和塔拉谁都不吭声。

塔拉紧紧地攥着石头，琢磨着河水是怎样把石头磨平、擦亮的。

等她冷静了一会，她说道："是我发现的石头！帕科要把石头抢走。就是他错了，和我没关系。"

"有，就怪你！"帕科态度也很强硬，"我只是想看看太阳照着石头是什么样子，你都不让我看。我看见你对着阳光看石头了！我只是想好好

---

decide *v.* 决定
polish *v.* 擦光

apologize *v.* 道歉
calm down 平静下来

◆ THE BLACK STONES

what they looked like when the sun was shining on them. I saw you holding them up to the light! All I wanted to do was *examine* them."

"They're mine!" Tala shouted.

Mrs. Yates closed her eyes to gather her thoughts—their fighting was making her *weary* and very, very sad.

Volcanoes and Magic

"Your *constant* arguments make me very unhappy," Mrs. Yates said softly. "You're brother and sister, and even twins. You could be best friends for your whole life if you would only try a little harder to get along. Will you try?"

Tala and Paco stared silently at the river. Mrs. Yates could tell by the way their jaws *tightened* and their backs tensed that they had no

---

看看。"

"石头是我的！"塔拉嚷道。

耶茨太太闭上了眼睛，屏气凝神——孩子们的争吵让她感到厌烦，而且非常伤心。

火山与魔法

"你们吵个没完，妈妈非常不高兴，"耶茨太太轻声说道，"你们是姐弟俩，还是双胞胎。只要你们俩好好相处，就能成为一辈子最好的朋友。你们就不能试试？"

塔拉和帕科谁也不说话，眼睛都盯着小河。耶茨太太看见他们俩下巴紧绷，后背僵硬，就知道他们谁也不想努力好好相处，至少现在不想，可能一辈子都不想。

---

examine *v.* 检查；仔细研究
constant *adj.* 持续不断的；重复的

weary *adj.* 感到厌烦的
tighten *v.* 使变紧

intention of trying to get along now, or ever.

She sighed and held out her hand. "Give me the stones, Tala," she said.

"But it's not fair," Tala whined. "I found them, not Paco. They're mine." Mrs. Yates waited. Tala's lips were *rigid* with anger, but she dropped the shiny black stones into her mother's hand.

"It's okay to be angry," her mother said. "Sometimes life doesn't seem fair at all. Everyone feels that way from time to time, but someday you'll learn that sharing makes you feel better than having a full pocket. You've heard the saying, 'It's better to give than to receive,' haven't you? Well, it's true."

Tala *folded* her arms and felt her whole body *stiffen*. She was furious. After all, she'd found the stones, hadn't she? So why was

---

她叹了口气，伸出一只手，"塔拉，把石头给我。"她说。

"这不公平，"塔拉满腹怨气地说，"是我找到的，不是帕科。石头是我的。"耶茨太太就一直等在那里。塔拉气得紧抿着嘴唇，但还是把闪亮的黑石丢到了妈妈的手心里。

"生气是很正常的，"妈妈说，"生活有时就是不公平的。每个人都会经历这种感觉，但是有一天你会明白，与人分享比独自拥有要快乐得多。你没听过那句谚语吗，'与其索取，不如奉献'。确实是这样。"

塔拉双手抱在胸前，感觉身体僵在那里。她真是怒火中烧。不管怎么说，都是她发现的石头啊，不是吗？为什么妈妈要讲什么奉献、分享呢？

---

rigid *adj.* 身体僵直的；呆住的   fold *v.* 交叉；交叠（双手或双臂）
stiffen *v.* 变得僵硬；变得紧张

◆ THE BLACK STONES

her mother talking about giving and sharing?

A moment later, Mrs. Yates told them both to hold out their hands as she dropped one stone onto each child's *outstretched* palm. Then she led Tala and Paco up the trail and home for dinner.

Tala and Paco may have been twins, but they were very different. Tala looked at the world as a scientist so everything was a question. She wanted to know why the sky turned orange at sunset and how a seashell created an *echo*. Paco, on the other hand, saw the world as a *magical* place filled with poems waiting to be written. Paco marveled at the beauty of an orange sunset and the mystery of a

---

过了一会儿，妈妈让他们俩都把手伸出来，往每个人的手心里放了一块石头。然后，她就领着两个孩子走上小路，回家吃饭去了。

塔拉和帕科虽然是双胞胎，但他们没有一个地方是相似的。塔拉总以科学家的眼光看待世界，所以对任何事物都带有疑问。她想弄清楚为什么日落时天空会变成橙色，还有贝壳里是怎样产生回音的。而帕科眼中的世界却是神奇的地方，还有未完成的诗篇等待着他去创作。橙色的日落之美与贝壳的回音之谜，都让帕科感叹世界无比神奇。

---

outstretched *adj.* 张开的；伸开的　　　　echo *n.* 回声；回响
magical *adj.* 奇妙的；神奇的

GROWING PAINS IV

seashell's echo.

Paco wondered if his stone could lead him into magical worlds. Maybe if he *rubbed* it three times, a genie would appear. Or perhaps it was a goodluck charm that would *protect* him all his life.

When Tala looked at her glassy stone, questions bubbled up inside her mind. How long had the stone been there? How old was it? Had it been formed by hot *lava* spewing out of a *volcano*?

Of course the twins argued about what it was, and what it wasn't, and who was right and who was wrong, and...

"STOP IT!" Mrs. Yates shouted when she just couldn't listen to

---

帕科想知道，他的石头是否能带他进入魔法世界。也许他只要擦三下石头，就会出现精灵；也许出现的是护身符，可以庇护他一生无忧。

塔拉看着晶莹剔透的石头，脑子里则浮现出一连串的问题——这块石头在河里多久了？它有多少年历史？这块石头是由火山喷发出的热岩浆形成的吗？

毫无悬念，这对双胞胎又争论起这石头究竟是什么，不是什么，谁说对了，谁说错了，还有……

"都闭嘴！"耶茨太太喊道，她实在是一分钟也听不下去了。

---

rub *v.* 揉；搓　　　　　　　　　　　protect *v.* 保护
lava *n.* （火山）熔岩　　　　　　　volcano *n.* 火山

them for one more minute.

"But it's a volcanic glass rock!" Tala *insisted*. "I know it *spewed* out from inside the earth!"

"You're wrong!" Paco hollered. "It's a magical good-luck stone!"

Mrs. Yates *groaned* and led the twins to the computer. She sat down between them and turned it on.

The Experiment

As the computer booted up, the twins started to argue about what *website* they would access first, but their mother stopped them.

"May I ask the two of you for a favor?" she said.

The twins waited.

"但这就是火山玻璃石！"塔拉毫不让步，"我知道，它是从地球里喷发出来的！"

"才不是呢！"帕科也喊道，"这是块有法力的幸运石！"

耶茨太太无奈地叹了一口气，领着两个孩子来到电脑前。她坐在两个孩子中间，启动了电脑。

实验

电脑启动时，这对双胞胎又开始争论他们应该先查哪个网站，妈妈只好再次叫他们安静下来。

"你们俩可不可以帮我一个忙？"妈妈问道。

两个孩子等着妈妈继续说下去。

---

insist *v.* 坚持
groan *v.* 叹息；呻吟
spew *v.* 喷出
website *n.* 网站

GROWING PAINS IV

"I would like you to do an *experiment*, as a gift to me. Just this once, I would like you both to research your stones without arguing. I'll work with you to find the answers, but no fighting. I want you to understand that life is much more peaceful if you work together to solve your problems. Okay?"

Tala and Paco looked at each other for several seconds, and then they *shrugged*. "Okay," they *reluctantly* agreed.

"What do you think we should search for first?" Mrs. Yates asked.

"I know what we should do!" Paco announced. "We should..."

Paco glanced at his mother, and the sad look on her face made him hesitate. Maybe there was a better way to *approach* this experiment.

"我想让你们俩做一个实验，就当作是送给我的礼物。就这一次，我希望你们俩不要争吵，安静地研究一下石头。我会和你们一起找到答案，但是在这个过程中不准打架。希望你们能明白，如果你们齐心协力解决问题的话，生活就会很平静。你们俩愿意吗？"

塔拉和帕科对视了几秒，然后都耸了耸肩膀，"好吧。"他们俩很不情愿地同意了。

"那你们觉得应该先查什么？"妈妈问他们。

"我知道查什么！"帕科大声说道，"我们应该……"

帕科瞥了妈妈一眼，看到妈妈有点伤心，不敢再说下去了。应该有更好的方法来进行这项实验。

---

experiment *n.* 实验
reluctantly *adv.* 不情愿地；勉强地
shrug *v.* 耸肩
approach *v.* 处理；对待

◆ THE BLACK STONES

"You can decide," he said to his sister.

"Maybe we should search for the name of our stones," Tala *suggested*. "Let's type the words volcanic glass into the *search engine* and see what websites come up."

"I don't care about volcanoes!" Paco said. "Let's type in good-luck stones."

"Volcanic glass!"

"Good-luck stones!"

Mrs. Yates put a *gentle* hand on each of their shoulders. When they were quiet, she made a suggestion.

"How about both?" she said. "And how about we *add* where you found the stones as well?" She typed the words volcanic glass

---

"你说吧。"他对妹妹说。

"我们可以先查查这种石头叫什么,"塔拉说,"可以在搜索栏里输入'火山玻璃',看看哪些网站有相关信息。"

"我才不管什么火山呢!"帕科又说,"应该输入'好运石'。"

"火山玻璃!"

"好运石!"

耶茨太太轻轻地把手放在两个孩子的肩头。等他们安静下来,她出了个主意。

"两个一起查怎么样?"她问道,"再把你们发现石头的地点也输入进去,好吧?"她在搜索栏里输入"火山玻璃好运阿帕奇飞跃山",然后

---

suggest *v.* 建议
gentle *adj.* 温和的;轻柔的

search engine 搜索引擎
add *v.* 增加;增添

GROWING PAINS IV

good luck Apache Leap Mountain into the search engine and waited to see what would happen. Mrs. Yates knew that the narrower the search, the more likely they were to get the results they wanted.

When their search results appeared, Paco and Tala studied them together. One of the short website *descriptions* mentioned nearly all of the *terms* they used to search.

"Let's go to that one," the twins said at exactly the same time.

Paco and Tala looked at each other in *amazement*. They had agreed on something, and even they were surprised.

"Is it okay if I hit the Enter key?" Paco asked.

"That's not fair!" Tala said. "You always get to..."

等着搜索结果。耶茨太太知道，搜索的范围越窄，就越可能查到想要的信息。

搜索结果出来以后，帕科和塔拉一起研究起来。有一段很短的网站描述几乎涵盖了他们输入的所有关键词。

"看这个网站。"两人异口同声地说道。

帕科和塔拉惊讶地看着对方。他们竟然有意见相同的时候，这异口同声把他们自己都吓了一跳。

"是不是按'确定'键就可以了？"帕科问。

"不公平！"塔拉说，"你总是抢着……"

---

description *n.* 描述
amazement *n.* 惊奇；诧异

term *n.* 术语；措辞

◆ **THE BLACK STONES**

Tala was about to say that Paco always got to do everything, but the look on her mother's face caused her to pause. She sat back and nodded to her brother. Paco pushed the Enter key and waited for the website about the volcanic goodluck stones to *load*.

As the website was loading, the phone rang and Mrs. Yates went to answer it, leaving Tala and Paco alone without their mother to *referee*. They both *wondered* if they could get along without her.

Searching for Answers

The website showed a picture of rocks that looked similar to the shiny stones Tala found. Paco and Tala *compared* their stones to the ones on the page in front of them and grinned.

塔拉想说，帕科总是什么事都抢在前面。但是看到妈妈的神情，她话说了一半就闭嘴了。她坐回原处，冲她哥哥点了点头。帕科用力按下了"确定"键，等着这个网站加载有关火山好运石的信息。

网站加载信息的时候，电话响了。耶茨太太起身去接电话，暂时不当塔拉和帕科的裁判了，留他们俩单独待在那。两个孩子都不确定，妈妈不在身边，他们是不是又得吵起来。

寻找答案

这个网站上出现了一幅石头的图片，图片里的石头看起来和塔拉发现的亮闪闪的石头很像。帕科和塔拉拿自己的石头和网页上的石头对比了一番，然后不由地笑了起来。

---

load *v.* 把（信息）输入（计算机） 　　referee *n.* 裁判员
wonder *v.* 想知道；想弄明白 　　　　compare *v.* 比较；对比

GROWING PAINS IV

"That's our stone!" they said, at *exactly* the same time.

The twins sat up straight and read the words on the *monitor* together.

"I told you!" Tala shouted, poking her brother. "Our stones came from inside the earth. They are called *obsidian* and were spewed out from a volcano. So I'm right!"

Paco was too busy reading a different part of the page to listen to his sister and when he was finished, he said, "I'm right! I told you these stones were good-luck stones!"

"See THAT?" Tala said, as she pointed to a word on the part of the page she was reading. Paco followed her finger to the words volcanic glass and read that part of the page. Then he focused his sister's *attention* on the word good luck and watched as she read.

"就是我们的石头！"他们又一次异口同声地说。

这对双胞胎坐直身体，一起读着电脑显示屏上的信息。

"我说的没错吧！"塔拉用手指戳着她哥哥，大喊道，"我们的石头是从地球里面出来的，名叫'黑曜石'，是从火山里喷发出来的。所以，我是对的！"

帕科正忙着读网页上的另一段话，没空儿理他妹妹。等他读完了，也说道："我说对了！我就说这些石头是好运石嘛！"

"看到那没？"塔拉指着网页上她读过的那一段问着哥哥。帕科看到了妹妹指着的"火山玻璃"一词，然后他把那一段读完了。他又让妹妹仔细看有"好运"这个词的段落，然后看着妹妹仔细读那段话。

---

exactly　*adv.*　恰好地；正好　　　　　monitor　*n.*　显示屏
obsidian　*n.*　黑曜石　　　　　　　　attention　*n.*　注意力；关注

◆ THE BLACK STONES

"It looks as if we were both right," Paco said.

"I know," his sister agreed. "These stones are probably thousands of years old, they came from inside the earth, and they have brought good luck to many, many people."

"Let's read more about the *legend* of the Apache Tears," Paco said. "It doesn't explain much on this page."

"I guess we should do some more research," Tala suggested.

The twins went back to the search page, typed in Apache Tears, and waited as several results came up. One website mentioned the Pinal Apache, which was a name given to a band of Apache from near Superior, Arizona, where Tala and Paco lived.

"看起来咱们都对了。"帕科说。

"我知道了，"他的妹妹也赞成这个结论，"这些石头可能有几千年的历史了，它们是从地球里面出来的，它们也给很多很多人带来了好运。"

"我们读一读'阿帕奇泪石'的传说吧，"帕科说，"这个网页上没有讲传说的事。"

"那我们应该多查一些东西。"塔拉提议说。

两个孩子回到搜索页，输入"阿帕奇泪石"，然后搜索到了几个相关网站。有一个网站提到了"皮纳尔·阿帕奇"，是一群阿帕奇人的名字，他们就住在塔拉和帕科家所在的亚利桑那州苏必利尔附近。

---

legend *n.* 传奇；传说

GROWING PAINS IV

"Let's try that one," Paco said, and when his sister agreed he was happily surprised—a nice feeling.

This webpage showed an *illustration* of an Apache *warrior*. Tala and Paco read the poem on the webpage slowly and *carefully*, and when they were finished they read it again.

Paco noticed that his sister was rubbing her stone between her fingers as she read, and he wondered if she was making a wish. Tala didn't usually like legends. She enjoyed reading about science. But Paco could tell that his sister was very interested in this story.

Paco decided that he would read more about volcanoes and all the rocks that were inside the earth, and he would try to understand how the river changed rocks to *smooth* stones.

"看看这个网站吧。"帕科说。塔拉同意了,这让帕科感到很惊喜——这种感觉真是不错。

这个网页上有一幅阿帕奇勇士的插图。塔拉和帕科很慢很认真地把网页上的诗读了一遍,读完之后又从头读了一遍。

帕科注意到塔拉读诗的同时在指间摩擦着石头,不知道她是不是在许愿。塔拉从来都不相信什么传说。她相信科学,喜欢科学读物。但是帕科确定,塔拉对这个故事非常感兴趣。

帕科决定要多读读有关火山的知识,还要多了解地球上的各种石头。他要弄清楚河水是怎样把岩石打磨成光滑的鹅卵石的。

---

illustration *n.* 插图
carefully *adv.* 仔细地;小心地
warrior *n.* 勇士
smooth *adj.* 光滑的

◆ THE BLACK STONES

For now, Paco and Tala decided to write down their own version of the legend so that they would have it to remember.

The Legend of the Apache Tears

Long, long ago, before the white men came, the Apaches *roamed* free. But a time came when the white men began to move west in search of new land. Hoping to protect their lands, Apache warriors came out to meet them, but the Apaches were no match for the white men. The white men killed many Apache warriors, and some were driven to the edge of a *cliff*. Rather than be captured, the warriors jumped from the cliff to their deaths. The Apache women heard of their warriors' deaths, and their *sadness* was deep and they were filled with great pain. Their *despair* was so complete that the

---

此刻，帕科和塔拉决定写下他们自己版本的泪石传说，这也可以留作以后的回忆。

阿帕奇泪石的传说

在很久很久以前，白人到来之前，阿帕奇人可以自由徜徉。但是后来，白人开始西进寻找新的土地。阿帕奇人为了保护自己的土地，与白人短兵相接，但他们根本不是白人的对手。白人杀害了很多阿帕奇勇士，活着的阿帕奇人一直被逼到悬崖边上。这些勇士宁死不屈，纵身跳下了悬崖。阿帕奇妇女听闻勇士们的死讯，悲痛欲绝。上帝将绝望之至的女人们

---

roam *v.* 漫步；游荡
sadness *v.* 悲伤

cliff *n.* 悬崖
despair *n.* 绝望

GROWING PAINS IV

◆ THE BLACK STONES

Great Father *embedded* their tears into the black stones that rested in the river.

Whoever carries these stones will have good luck always. And whoever keeps these stones close will never again cry tears, for the Apache women have cried tears in their place.

Paco and Tala sat back and studied their stones in silence. They raised them to the light and gazed into their centers. They thought about the women who had cried for their men, and they felt sad. Then they *shut down* the computer and *clenched* their stones tight.

When their mother returned, they told her the Legend of the Apache Tears.

的眼泪注入了小河中的黑色石头里。

带着这些石头的人一生都将有好运相伴。贴身留着这些石头的人永远不会再流泪，因为阿帕奇妇女已经替他们把眼泪流完了。

帕科和塔拉坐了回去，默默地看着他们的石头。他们把石头对着光，凝神看着中心部分。他们想到那些妇女们为丈夫痛哭流泪的情景，不觉伤心起来。后来，两人关掉了电脑，紧紧地攥住石头。

妈妈回来了，孩子们给她讲了阿帕奇泪石的传说。

---

embed *v.* 使嵌入

clench *v.* 握紧；攥紧（拳头）

shut down 关闭

"Can you see the tear of an Apache woman?" Paco asked her, as he held his stone up to the light.

Mrs. Yates took the stone and let the light *filter* through it. "I think I do see it," she said. "It's a tear for her man, and it's a tear for the sad children he left behind. It's a tear that says 'I wish my children were happy.' "

Paco and Tala understood that she was not just thinking about the Apache children in the legend. She was thinking about them. They understood that their mother wanted them to be happy, but they also knew that they couldn't *promise* not to fight with each other. They were, after all, brother and sister.

"你能看见阿帕奇女人的眼泪吗？"帕科把他的那块石头举起来对着光，让妈妈去看。

耶茨太太拿过石头，看着光线从石头中穿过。"我觉得我真的看到了，"她说，"这滴眼泪是为她丈夫流的，也是为丈夫留给她的难过的孩子们流的。这滴眼泪在说'希望我的孩子们都能幸福快乐。'"

帕科和塔拉明白妈妈不只是在想传说中的阿帕奇孩子们，她在想自己的孩子。他们明白妈妈希望他们幸福，但同时也知道他们不能保证从此不再吵架。但不管怎么说，他们都是亲兄妹。

---

filter　*v.* 隐约透过　　　　　　　　　　　promise　*v.* 承诺；保证

◆ THE BLACK STONES

That night, after talking it over, Paco and Tala gave their stones to their mother. At first, Mrs. Yates *refused* to take them since the stones seemed to have made her children friends again. Eventually, Paco and Tala *convinced* her that they wanted her to have the Apache Tears. Mrs. Yates slept with the obsidian stones under her pillow that night, and the next day she went to the jeweler and had them made into a *necklace*. When the necklace was ready, she slipped it on and never took it off again. Apache Tears had indeed brought them good luck!

那天晚上,帕科和塔拉商量了一下,决定把两块石头都交给妈妈。开始,耶茨太太觉得是这两块石头使孩子们和平相处,所以不想要他们的石头。但最终,她明白两个孩子是想让她带着阿帕奇泪石。耶茨太太当天晚上把这两块黑曜石放在枕头下,第二天她就去珠宝店把石头做成了项链。项链做好以后,她马上戴在脖子上,再也没拿下来过。因为阿帕奇泪石确实给他们带来了好运!

---

refuse *v.* 拒绝　　　　　　　　　　convince *v.* 使相信;使确信
necklace *n.* 项链

GROWING PAINS IV

7

Only One Aunt Maggie

Aunt Maggie Is Coming!

"Guess who called today to say she is due for a visit?" Adam's mom *squealed*. Before Adam or his dad had time to guess, Adam's mom answered her own question. "My sister! Aunt Maggie is coming this weekend!"

"Whooo-hooo!" Adam chanted, waving his arms over his head.

"Well, I can see you're *terribly* upset over this news," Dad *chuckled*, serving himself salad.

只有一个玛姬姨妈

玛姬姨妈来了!

"猜猜今天谁打电话说要来看我们?"亚当的妈妈尖叫着。亚当和爸爸还没来得及猜,妈妈就脱口而出她的答案:"我的姐姐!你的玛姬姨妈这个周末要来!"

"哇呼!"亚当双手举过头顶,欢呼起来。

"哦,这个消息让你'苦不堪言'是吧。"爸爸偷笑着,边说边给自己盛了些沙拉。

---

squeal　v.　发出长而尖的叫声　　　　　　terribly　adv.　非常;极度
chuckle　v.　偷笑;低声轻笑

◆ ONLY ONE AUNT MAGGIE

That evening, the Wiles family laughed up a storm sharing Aunt Maggie stories.

"Remember last year when Aunt Maggie came into my second-grade class and helped us bake a three-foot high volcano cake—that *erupted*?" Adam recalled.

"Or the time she got all of us to do that *ridiculous* cheer at your soccer game?" added Dad.

There was one thing that the Wiles family knew for sure—Aunt Maggie was the most fun person they knew.

Summon Your Building Partner!

When Aunt Maggie arrived on Friday, she eagerly unpacked toys from her *recent* trip to Russia and her latest picture book that she wrote and illustrated. Then she cupped her hands to her mouth and announced, "It's fort time—summon your building partner!"

　　当晚，怀尔斯全家（怀尔斯为亚当一家人的姓）欢声笑语不断，讲着玛姬姨妈的故事。
　　"记得去年我二年级的时候，玛姬姨妈到教室帮我们烤那个三英尺高的火山蛋糕吗，它居然'喷发'了！"亚当回忆道。
　　"还有那次她让我们在你的足球赛上呐喊加油，真是傻透了！"爸爸补充说。
　　有件事怀尔斯一家深信不疑——玛姬姨妈是他们认识的最有趣的人。
　　召唤你的同盟！
　　星期五，玛姬姨妈一到就迫不及待地拿出最近从俄罗斯旅行带回来的玩具和她最新的图画书，文字与插图都是出自她手。然后她双手握成喇叭状，大声宣布道："现在是修筑碉堡时间——召唤你的同盟吧！"

---

erupt *v.* 爆发；喷发　　　　　　　　ridiculous *adj.* 可笑的
summon *v.* 召唤　　　　　　　　　　recent *adj.* 最近的

GROWING PAINS IV

◆ ONLY ONE AUNT MAGGIE

"Yahooo!" roared Adam, running to call Dario, who lived next door.

An hour later, Aunt Maggie and the boys built a pillow, *cushion*, and blanket fort *spanning* two rooms. "We said we'd break last year's fort record—and we did!" Dario proudly *announced*.

A Day of Painting and Baking

The next morning, Adam made his Saturday morning *specialty*—buckwheat pancakes with bananas.

After breakfast, Dario came over for a day of painting and baking. Aunt Maggie taught the boys a fancy brush stroke for making realistic-looking clouds.

"耶！"亚当欢呼着跑去叫隔壁的达里奥。

一个小时后，玛姬姨妈和孩子们用枕头、坐垫和毯子建起了跨越两个房间的碉堡。"我们说过要打破去年的碉堡纪录——我们成功了！"达里奥自豪地宣布。

绘画和烘焙之日

第二天早上，亚当做了周六特色早餐——香蕉荞麦薄饼。

吃过早餐后，达里奥也来加入了绘画和烘焙之日。玛姬姨妈教孩子们用一种奇特的笔法来画出逼真的云朵。

---

cushion *n.* 坐垫；垫子
announce *v.* 宣布

span *v.* 跨越
specialty *n.* 特色菜；特色食品

GROWING PAINS IV

After lunch, the *trio* baked a *racetrack* cake—topped with race cars from Adam's car collection!

"Your aunt is so cool," Dario told Adam before heading home for dinner.

Aunt Maggie's Travel Stories

After dinner at Adam's house, the family gathered to hear Aunt Maggie's travel stories. The family room was set up like a theater, with Aunt Maggie seated in a chair facing her *audience*. Everyone's eyes *were glued to* Aunt Maggie as she spoke, and everyone's hands were busy popping grapes in their mouths.

吃过午饭，三个人烤了一个赛车道蛋糕——蛋糕上还特地放置了亚当收藏的赛车模型！

"你的姨妈实在是太酷了！"达里奥对亚当抛下这句评语，然后回家吃饭去了。

玛姬姨妈的旅行故事

亚当一家人吃过晚餐后，聚在一起听玛姬姨妈讲旅行故事。整个客厅被布置得像剧场一样，玛姬姨妈坐在椅子上，面向观众。玛姬姨妈讲述的时候，所有人都目不转睛地盯着她，边听边忙着往嘴里扔葡萄。

---

trio *n.* 三人组合　　　　　　　　racetrack *n.* 赛车道；跑马场
audience *n.* 观众；听众　　　　　be glued to 聚精会神地盯着

◆ ONLY ONE AUNT MAGGIE

"Can I get anyone more grapes?" Adam's mom asked between stories.

"No, thank you," said Aunt Maggie. "But do you have any chips?"

"Not today," mom *replied*.

"Well, you know me," said Aunt Maggie, pulling a bag of chips from her tote. "I never leave home without my two favorite foods, chocolate and chips!"

Then she told of an ice *sculpture* festival where she saw an ice lion as tall as the ceiling. And an ice *castle* as big as the house!

Is She Okay?

The next morning, Aunt Maggie *accompanied* Adam and Dario to the park six blocks away.

"我再去拿些葡萄吧？"亚当的妈妈在故事的间歇问道。

"不用了，谢谢。"玛姬姨妈说，"但是能拿点薯条吗？"

"现在没有啊。"妈妈回答说。

"呵呵，你知道，"玛姬姨妈边说边从手提袋里拖出一袋薯条，"我总是随身携带两种至爱美食——巧克力和薯条！"

接着她讲到了冰雕节，她在那里看见了高及屋顶的冰狮子，还有大如房子的冰雕城堡。

她没事吧?

第二天早上，玛姬姨妈陪亚当和达里奥去了六个街区以外的公园。

---

reply *v.* 回答
castle *n.* 城堡

sculpture *n.* 雕塑品；雕刻作品
accompany *v.* 陪伴

GROWING PAINS IV

"Whew... how much longer, kiddos?" Aunt Maggie asked, wiping her damp brow.

"Just three more *blocks*," answered Adam. He noticed that she was sweating a lot for a cool day and that her face was quite red.

"Your aunt looks as if she just ran a marathon—is she okay?" Dario *whispered* to Adam. Adam wasn't so sure.

When they reached the park, Aunt Maggie sat on a bench. When she caught her breath, she took out *a* small *handful of* colored chocolates and called out, "Chocolate, anyone? I sure need a sweet *treat* after all that exercise!"

"哟……还有多远才到，小伙子们？"玛姬姨妈一边擦额头的汗一边问。

"还有三条街就到了。"亚当回答道。他注意到玛姬姨妈在这个凉爽的天气里出了很多汗，而且脸通红。

"你的姨妈看起来好像刚跑完一场马拉松，她没事吧？"达里奥在亚当耳边轻声说。亚当也不方便确认。

他们一到公园，玛姬姨妈就一屁股坐在长凳上。她歇了口气之后，拿出一小把五颜六色的巧克力，大声叫道："有人要巧克力吗？激烈的运动后我可是要给自己一点'甜头'。"

---

block *n.* 街区
a handful of 一把

whisper *v.* 低声说；悄悄说
treat *n.* 款待

◆ ONLY ONE AUNT MAGGIE

On the way home, Aunt Maggie breathed even heavier and walked even slower. When the boys *questioned* her about being so tired, she explained, "Well, I'm overweight and out of shape. So now a ten-minute walk can really wipe me out! In fact, I'm going to lie down when we get home, kiddos."

Adam's Thoughts *Drift* to Science Class

As the boys made turkey sandwiches for lunch, Dario talked about dog tricks he was learning. But Adam's thoughts kept drifting to science class. And it was Saturday!

"*Remember* when Ms. Scott told us that the heart is a *muscle* that needs exercise just like other muscles?" Adam spoke slowly.

回家的路上，玛姬姨妈的呼吸比去时更加沉重，脚步也愈发缓慢。当孩子们问她为什么这么累时，她回答说："我都胖得没有样儿了，现在走十分钟的路就能要了我的命！说句实话，小伙子们，我一进家门就得累趴下。"

亚当的思绪飘到了科学课上

孩子们为午饭准备火鸡三明治时，达里奥念叨着他正在学的逗狗的把戏。但亚当满脑子出现的都是科学课。这可是周六啊！

"记得斯科特老师在什么时候告诉我们心脏也是肌肉组织，就像其他肌肉组织一样需要锻炼吗？"亚当缓缓地说，"记得她当时让我们看的那

---

question *v.* 询问；向……提出问题
remember *v.* 记得；记起

drift *v.* 飘移；漂流
muscle *n.* 肌肉

GROWING PAINS IV

"And remember when she showed us that picture of *arteries clogged with fat*?"

"Yeah," said Dario.

"Well, I think that must be how Aunt Maggie's arteries look, which means that it's harder for blood to get to her heart, which is not a good thing," Dario said, frowning.

Adam couldn't imagine anything bad happening to Aunt Maggie. "We've got to do something, but what? What can we do?" Adam crunched on a carrot, eyebrows *furrowed*.

"You know, my dad lost about 25 pounds last year," shared Dario. "His doctor told him that if he didn't, he could get heart disease."

"Really?" Adam asked, *leaning* in. "How did he do it?"

张被脂肪堵住的动脉血管的照片吗？"

"记得。"达里奥说。

"哎，我觉得玛姬姨妈的动脉血管一定也是那样的。那样的话血液就更难到达她的心脏，那样的话就糟了。"达里奥说着，也皱起了眉头。

亚当不敢想象玛姬姨妈遭遇任何不幸。"我们得做点什么，但是做什么呢？我们能怎么做？"亚当嚼着一根胡萝卜，眉头紧锁地说。

"你知道吗，我爸爸去年减了差不多25磅。"达里奥告诉亚当，"医生说如果他体重没减这么多的话，就有可能得心脏病。"

"真的？"亚当身子往前倾了一些，问道："他怎么减掉的？"

---

artery *n.* 动脉　　　　　　　　　　clog *v.* 阻塞；堵塞
furrow *v.* （眉）皱起　　　　　　　lean *v.* （身体）倾斜

◆ ONLY ONE AUNT MAGGIE

GROWING PAINS IV

"Well, he started walking Buddy after dinner every night. And he *actually* eats a lot of the same meals as before, but now my mom makes them with healthier *ingredients*." Dario explained how his mom now makes cheeseburgers—one of his dad's favorites— with wheat buns, lean beef, low-fat cheese, and tomato slices.

"Yeah, my mom makes brown rice now instead of white rice," added Dario. "And she buys wheat bread instead of white bread. It's not so bad once you get used to it."

"Also, no more doughnuts for breakfast or chips with lunch. Now our family only eats that kind of food on Junk Food Fridays for Game Night."

"Ooohh! Junk Food Fridays sound cool," said Adam.

"他每天晚饭后就去遛我家的狗巴迪。虽然他吃的饭菜和以前差不多，但是我妈妈现在都是用更健康的原料做菜。"达里奥解释道。他爸爸最喜欢吃奶酪汉堡包，他妈妈现在用馒头、瘦牛肉、低脂奶酪和西红柿来做给爸爸吃。

"不错，我妈妈现在也用糙米做饭，不用精白米。"达里奥补充道，"买小麦面包，不买白面包。习惯之后也就觉得，其实并不是那么难以下咽。"

"而且，早餐不再有甜甜圈，午餐不再有炸薯条。现在我们家只在星期五晚上的'游戏之夜'才吃这些东西，我们把那天叫'垃圾食品日'。"

"天哪，星期五'垃圾食品日'，听起来挺新鲜！"亚当说。

---

actually *adv.* 的确；事实上   ingredient *n.* 原料；成分

Let's Do It!

"So your dad *lost weight* by walking the dog after dinner and eating junk food once a week instead of every day," Adam thought aloud. "And he ate healthier ingredients in his favorite meals, right?"

"Yup," said Dario.

"Well, if your dad can do it, so can Aunt Maggie!" Adam exclaimed. "We can tell her how he did it so she can do it, too."

"Like make her a chart, or something?" asked Dario.

"Great idea! Let's do it!" Adam said, heading out the door. "Is your dad home? We'll need his help."

Dario grabbed his hat and followed Adam. "Let's do it!" he called to Adam's back.

行动起来！

"就是说你爸爸每天晚饭后遛狗，一周吃一次垃圾食品，不能天天吃，就减肥成功了？"亚当自言自语道，"他还是可以吃喜欢的东西，只不过是原料更健康，对吗？"

"没错。"达里奥说。

"太好了！既然你爸爸能做到，玛姬姨妈也能做到。"亚当兴奋地说，"我们可以告诉她你爸爸减肥的方法，她也可以瘦下来的。"

"给她列个表之类的吧？"达里奥问。

"好主意！开始吧！"亚当边说着边向门外走去，"你爸爸在家吗？我们需要他帮忙。"

达里奥抓起帽子，跟上亚当的步子。"开始干吧！"他在亚当身后喊道。

---

lose weight 减肥；减轻体重

GROWING PAINS IV

Adam, Dario, and Dario's dad listened to the baseball game on the radio as they created the *poster*. Along the top of the white poster board, Dario drew funny pictures of Aunt Maggie making faces while lifting weights and power walking.

Below the illustrations, Adam wrote a list of less healthy foods in one *column*, like white flour tortillas, hot dogs, and mashed potatoes. And Dario's dad wrote the healthier *alternative* in the other column, like wheat tortillas, soy dogs, and baked sweet potatoes.

When they finished, Dario's dad *dictated* to Adam a list of foods that he ate when he craved junk food. Along the bottom of the poster, Adam wrote, "If you crave crunchy chips, try some nuts,

---

亚当、达里奥和达里奥的爸爸一边听着收音机里的棒球节目，一边做海报。在白色海报板的顶端，达里奥画了一些玛姬姨妈一边举重或速走，一边做鬼脸的滑稽图片。

在图片下面，亚当在一栏中列出了不健康食品清单，比如白面玉米饼、热狗、土豆泥等等。达里奥的爸爸则在另一栏中列出了比较健康的替代食物清单，像小麦玉米饼、豆热狗、烤红薯等。

他们完成海报后，达里奥的爸爸还让亚当记下了一些食物，他自己实在想吃垃圾食品时就吃这些东西代替。亚当在海报底部写道，"如果你无法抵制脆薯条的诱惑，就吃些坚果、胡萝卜条和年糕吧。"如果你实在想

---

poster *n.* 海报　　　　　　　　　　　　column *n.* 栏
alternative *n.* 供选择的事物　　　　　dictate *v.* 口述

carrot sticks, or a rice cake. If you crave sweet chocolate, try a fruity yogurt, Jello, or dried fruit."

Tell Her What's in Your Heart

As Adam headed back to his house with the poster, he felt excited—and *nervous*, too. What if the poster makes Aunt Maggie angry? What should I say to her when I give her the poster?

After dinner, Adam went to his mom for advice. "Just tell her what's in your heart, Adam," she said.

That night when Aunt Maggie came by Adam's room to say goodnight, he handed her the poster. "Aunt Maggie, you are the coolest, funniest, most *amazing* grown-up Dario and I know. And we

---

吃甜巧克力，那就试着用酸奶、果冻、干果代替吧。"

告诉她你的想法

亚当拿着海报回家的时候，既兴奋又紧张——如果海报把玛姬姨妈惹生气了怎么办？当我把海报给她的时候我应该怎么说？

吃过饭后，亚当去向妈妈寻求建议。"直接告诉她你的想法吧，亚当，"妈妈说。

晚上，趁玛姬姨妈来房间给他道晚安的时候，他把海报递给了姨妈。"玛姬姨妈，你是我和达里奥认识的最酷、最有趣、最棒的长辈。我们给

---

nervous *adj.* 神经紧张的；担忧的   amazing *adj.* 令人惊奇的；惊人的

GROWING PAINS IV

made you this poster because we really love you and don't want anything bad to happen to your heart."

"My heart?" Aunt Maggie *repeated*, looking confused.

I Have Only One Me

As she read the poster, a happy tear *rolled down* her cheek. "Kiddo," she said. "Tonight I *pledge* to you and Dario that I will take this poster home with me, and I will follow it. Because after all, I only have one me, right?"

"Besides, this healthy food list doesn't look that bad. Now get to bed so you can take me to the airport in the morning. And Adam,

---

你画这幅海报是因为我们真的爱你,不希望你的心脏出任何问题。"

"我的心脏?"玛姬姨妈迷惑不解地重复了一遍。

只有一个我

读着海报,幸福的泪水从她脸庞滚落下来。"小伙子,今晚我向你和达里奥保证,我会把这张海报带回家并按照上面的做。因为毕竟,世上只有一个我,对吗?"

"而且,这个健康食物表看起来还不错。马上睡觉,明天上午你还得

---

repeat *v.* 重复
pledge *v.* 保证;许诺
roll down 滚落

◆ ONLY ONE AUNT MAGGIE

thank you, and Dario, too."

Three months later, Adam opened this letter from Aunt Maggie...

Dear Adam and Dario,

*I've already lost 12 pounds, thanks to your **excellent** poster!*

See you in two weeks, and get ready to build the biggest fort EVER!

*Love, The **Incredible Shrinking** Aunt Maggie*

送我去机场。谢谢你，亚当，还有达里奥。"

三个月后，亚当接到来自玛姬姨妈的信……

亲爱的亚当和达里奥：

我已经减掉了12磅，谢谢你们精彩的海报！

两周后见，准备做史上最大的碉堡吧！

爱你们的，正在飞速瘦身的

玛姬姨妈

---

excellent *adj.* 卓越的；极好的；优秀的
incredible *adj.* 难以置信的；惊人的
shrink *v.* 收缩；缩小

GROWING PAINS IV

8

The Ant in the Photograph

Tonight was Parents' Night for Mr. Casey's third-grade classroom. Daron was excited. He felt like a *balloon* filled close to *bursting*. He rushed through his favorite dinner. He did his math homework as fast as he could. He begged his mom to please let him walk the dog after Parents' Night. Finally, Daron and his mom arrived at school.

照片里的蚂蚁

今天晚上是凯西老师三年级班级的家长之夜。达龙兴奋得就好像是充满气即将要爆裂的气球。晚饭都是他爱吃的，他却只是匆匆忙忙地吃完了，然后又以最快的速度做完了数学作业。他乞求妈妈允许他在家长之夜结束后去遛狗。终于，达龙和妈妈到达了学校。

---

balloon *n.* 气球　　　　　　　　　　　　　　　　burst *v.* 爆裂；炸开

◆ THE ANT IN THE PHOTOGRAPH

"My project is right over there," Daron said, pulling his mom across the classroom. They wove around rows of desks then stopped in front of the art table.

"Here it is!" Daron proudly pointed to a sculpture of a *brightly* painted, *giant* ant. "I *recycled* stuff that was being thrown away like milk cartons and bottle caps. Can you tell that the legs are old toilet paper *tubes*?"

"You did a great job," Daron's mom said. "It's as colorful as a circus clown."

"Thanks. It took me almost a whole week to make it," Daron said.

"我的作品就在那边。"达龙边说,边拉着妈妈穿过教室。他们绕过一排排书桌,然后在艺术品展示桌前停了下来。

"就是这个!"达龙骄傲地指向一座鲜艳、巨大的蚂蚁雕塑。"我用那些可以循环再利用的废品,像牛奶纸盒和瓶盖之类的,做成了这个,你能看出来蚂蚁的腿是用旧的厕纸卷筒做的吗?"

"真是太棒了。"达龙的妈妈说道,"色彩鲜艳得就像一个马戏团小丑。"

"谢谢夸奖。我花了近一周的时间才完成的呢。"达龙说道。

brightly *adv.* 鲜艳地;明亮地
recycle *v.* 回收利用;循环利用

giant *adj.* 巨大的
tube *n.* 管;管状物

GROWING PAINS IV

Let's take a *photograph* of you with it," his mom said as she pulled her camera out of its blue bag. Daron *picked up* his ant, held it high, and grinned for the photograph.

"Be careful with that," his mom warned, placing the camera back in its bag. "I'm not ready to leave yet."

Daron put the ant down and followed his mom as she *toured* the room.

Returning to his ant, Daron said happily, "I can't wait to show my ant to Dad when he gets home from his business trip." He held his ant high and *admired* it. But in his excitement, Daron didn't notice a book on the floor. When he stepped on it, his feet flew out from under him as if he'd stepped on a banana peel. He and his ant

"来，让我给你们拍张照片吧。"妈妈一边说着，一边从蓝色相机套里拿出相机。达龙拿起蚂蚁雕塑，举得高高地，笑呵呵地拍下了这张照片。

"小心点儿！"妈妈边提醒着达龙，边把相机放回了套子里。"我还想再随处看看。"

达龙放下雕塑，跟着妈妈在教室里参观。

达龙又转回到了自己的蚂蚁雕塑前，高兴地说道："我迫不及待地想让爸爸在出差回来第一时间就看到我的作品。"他高高地举起蚂蚁雕塑欣赏着。可他光顾着高兴，没注意到地上有本书。他踩到了书，就好像踩到

photograph *n.* 照片
tour *v.* 参观；游览

pick up 拾起
admire *v.* 欣赏

◆ THE ANT IN THE PHOTOGRAPH

GROWING PAINS IV

crashed to the floor.

"Oh no, it's ruined!" Daron exclaimed when he saw pieces of his ant littering the floor. He picked up the flattened milk cartons, *twisted* straws, and ripped paper that had made up his ant. "There's no way I can fix it," he *moaned*, "and Dad never saw it."

"I'm sorry, Daron," his mom said, helping him pick up the last pieces of his ant.

"I hope the photograph of it turns out," said Daron.

"Good thinking," his mom replied. "Dad will like to see that." She put the last of the ant sculpture pieces in the *wastebasket*. "Are you ready to go? We can stop at the house, pick up the dog, and go to Elm Creek Park to walk him if you want."

了一块香蕉皮，脚底哧溜一滑。结果，他和蚂蚁雕塑都摔到了地上。

"哦，天哪，摔坏了！"达龙看到蚂蚁雕塑的碎片散落一地，尖叫了起来。他拾起了摔碎的雕塑零件：压平的牛奶纸盒，弄弯的吸管和撕碎的纸片。"没有办法补救了。"他抱怨道，"爸爸没机会看到蚂蚁雕塑了。"

"太可惜了，达龙。"妈妈一边说着一边帮他捡起其他的碎片。

"希望那张照片能帮上些忙。"达龙说道。

"好主意。爸爸一定很喜欢那张照片。" 妈妈回应道，并随手把最后一片雕塑碎片扔进了垃圾箱。"我们回去吧，好吗？我们可以去榆树溪公园遛遛狗，你还想去吗？"

---

twist *v.* 扭曲；弯曲变形　　　　　　　　　　**moan** *v.* 抱怨；发牢骚
wastebasket *n.* 废纸篓；垃圾箱

◆ THE ANT IN THE PHOTOGRAPH

"I guess," Daron said with a sad shrug.

The next afternoon, the school bell rang and kids piled out of the building. Daron followed the crowd toward the buses but stopped when he heard his name.

"Hi, Mom," he said when he *spied* her. "What are you doing here? Did you get the photograph from last night?"

"No, *unfortunately*, I can't find the camera," she said.

"But you're a mom, and you never lose things," Daron said.

"Maybe I left it at school last night," his mom said. "Will you help me search the lost and found?" But after digging through mountains of sweatshirts and sweaters, sorting through *mismatched* mittens and gloves, looking at socks, hats and *scarves*, they did not find the camera.

"也好。"达龙难过地耸了耸肩。

第二天下午，放学铃响了，孩子们从教学楼鱼贯而出。达龙跟随着队伍走向校车，突然听到有人喊他的名字，便停了下来。

"妈妈！"达龙在人群中看见了妈妈。"你怎么在这儿？昨晚的照片洗好了吗？"

"没有，太糟糕了，我找不到相机了。"妈妈说道。

"可妈妈你从来都不丢东西呀。"达龙说道。

"也许昨晚我把它落在学校了。"妈妈说道。"你和我去失物招领处找找好吗？"他们翻遍了一堆堆运动衫和毛衣，又将不匹配的手套整理出来，最后又看了看放袜子、帽子和围巾的地方，可是没有找到照相机。

---

spy *v.* 看见；发现
mismatch *v.* 使错配；不匹配

unfortunately *adv.* 不幸地；遗憾的是
scarf *n.* 围巾

GROWING PAINS IV

"Let's go to the office and ask whether anyone *turned* it *in*," Daron suggested, his voice filled with worry. But no one in the office had seen it either.

"What if we never find it, Mom?" Daron asked as they walked to the car. "You don't have your nice camera anymore, and I don't have a picture to show Dad."

"Well," his mom said *thoughtfully*, "I'll check the *apartment* one more time. If it's not there, we may just have to hope for the kindness of a stranger."

"Was our name and telephone number on the camera?" Daron asked.

"I don't remember," his mom answered. "I sure hope so."

"咱们还是去办公室问问吧，看有没有人捡到。"达龙建议道，声音里流露出担忧。遗憾的是，没有人捡到他们的相机。

"妈妈，如果我们永远都找不到，那可怎么办呢？"达龙边问边跟着妈妈向车子走去。"你再也用不了那部漂亮的相机了，而爸爸也看不到我的照片了。"

"好吧，"妈妈若有所思地说道，"我再回房间里找找。如果还是找不到，我们也只能期待有好心的陌生人捡到再还给我们了。"

"相机上有我们的名字和电话号码吗？"达龙问道。

"我不记得了，"妈妈回答道，"希望有吧。"

---

turn in 上交；提交　　　　　　　　thoughtfully *adv.* 沉思地
apartment *n.* 公寓房间；套房

◆ THE ANT IN THE PHOTOGRAPH

Daron sat at the kitchen table the next evening practicing spelling words with his mom when the telephone rang. He wrote a few words while he waited for her, but it was hard to *concentrate*. A *gloomy* cloud hung over his head. There was still no sign of the lost camera. He had tried to make another ant sculpture, but the whole thing fell apart when he started to paint it before the glue dried. Now he had run out of time. His dad was coming home tomorrow, and Daron had nothing to show him.

When his mom finished her *conversation* she made a quick call and then suggested they go outside for a while.

"I don't feel like it," Daron *muttered*.

第二天傍晚，达龙坐在餐桌前和妈妈一起练习拼写单词。这时，电话响了。妈妈接电话时，达龙写下了几个单词，但他满腹担忧，真的很难集中注意力。没有一点关于丢失的相机的线索。达龙也曾试图再做一个蚂蚁雕塑，可是胶还没干他就急着上色，弄得整个作品都碎掉了。现在他真的没有时间了。爸爸明天就回来了，达龙没有什么可以向爸爸展示的了。

妈妈接完电话，又很快地打了一个电话，然后她建议达龙和她一起出去走走。

"我不想去。"达龙小声地嘀咕道。

---

concentrate *v.* 集中（心思）；全神贯注
conversation *n.* 交谈；会话

gloomy *adj.* 沮丧的；忧伤的
mutter *v.* 轻声说话；咕哝抱怨

GROWING PAINS IV

Mom smiled and gently *tugged* Daron to the door. "Come on. A surprise is coming."

Daron *flopped* on the front steps and waited, but nothing happened. "This isn't a very good surprise, Mom," he sighed. "Can I go back inside?"

His mom laughed, "You'll miss the fun if you leave now, look."

An older boy riding a bike came toward them. "Are you Daron?" he asked.

"Yes," Daron answered slowly.

The boy got off his bike, put down his kickstand and *extended* his hand toward Daron. "Hi, I'm Michael." Daron *hesitated*, and then shook his hand. "I think this belongs to you," Michael said and

---

妈妈笑了，轻轻地把他拉到了门口。"走吧，惊喜正等着你呢。"

达龙重重地坐到了前门台阶上，等了一会，可是什么也没发生。"这不像是有什么意外惊喜呀，妈妈。"他叹了口气。"我能回去了吗？"

妈妈笑着说，"如果你现在离开，你将错过有趣的事。看，来了！"

一个比达龙大的男孩儿骑着自行车过来了。"你是达龙吗？"他问道。

"是的。"达龙慢慢地回答道。

男孩下了车，放下停车支架，向达龙伸出手。"你好，我叫迈克尔。"达龙迟疑了一下，然后和他握了握手。"这个是你的吧。"迈克尔

---

tug *v.* 用力拉；拽
extend *v.* 伸展；伸出（手臂等）

flop *v.* 猛然坐下；重重地坐下
hesitate *v.* 犹豫；迟疑

◆ **THE ANT IN THE PHOTOGRAPH**

GROWING PAINS Ⅳ

pulled a blue camera bag from his *handlebars*.

Daron's eyes opened wide, his jaw nearly fell to the front steps. "Our camera? Thanks! Where did you find it?"

"I found it in Elm Creek Park, by a park bench," Michael replied.

"I remember now," said Daron's mom, "we took a break from walking the dog and sat on a bench for a while. We must have forgotten to take the camera with us when we started walking again."

Daron unzipped the bag, pulled out the camera and turned it around, looking for something. "We don't have our name on this. How did you know it was ours?"

"I *discovered* that you and I have something in common," said

---

边说边从自行车把手上取下一个蓝色的相机包。

达龙瞪大了眼睛,张大了嘴巴,下巴几乎要掉到台阶上。"我们的相机?太感谢你了!你在哪里找到的?"

"榆树溪公园长椅旁边。"迈克尔回答道。

"我想起来了,"妈妈说道,"那晚我们去公园遛狗,坐在长椅上休息了一会儿。当我们起身离开的时候,一定把相机落在了那里。"

达龙拉开相机包,拿出相机,又翻来覆去地看了看,好像在找什么东西。"相机上没有我们的名字呀,你怎么知道这相机是我们的呢?"

"因为我发现我们有些共同之处。"迈克尔说道。达龙困惑地看了看

---

handlebar *n.* (自行车)车把;把手   discover *v.* (偶然)发现

◆ THE ANT IN THE PHOTOGRAPH

Michael. Daron gave Michael a *puzzled* look—he couldn't imagine having anything in common with this tall boy. Michael explained, "I printed the pictures in the camera hoping one of them would give me a clue about the people who owned the camera. I saw the one showing you in your classroom with your ant sculpture. And guess what?" Daron *shrugged* his shoulders. "We had the same third-grade teacher. I'm in tenth grade now, but I remember doing the same project in third grade. Mr. Casey always has his students make sculptures out of recycled stuff."

"Really?" Daron asked.

"But yours was better than mine. I made a dog, but the nose

迈克尔——他很难想象自己和眼前这个高个子男孩儿有什么共同之处。迈克尔解释道:"我把相机里的照片打印了出来,希望能找到些关于相机主人的线索。我看到一张照片,是你在教室里和你的蚂蚁雕塑的合影。你猜怎么着?"达龙耸耸肩。"我三年级的老师也是凯西老师。我现在上十年级了,但我仍记得上三年级的时候做过同样的活动。凯西老师总是让学生使用可回收的材料做些雕塑品。"

"真的吗?"达龙问道。

"不过,你比我做得好多了。我当时做了一条狗。可是鼻子太长了,

puzzled *adj.* 困惑的;迷惑的   shrug *v.* 耸肩

GROWING PAINS IV

◆ THE ANT IN THE PHOTOGRAPH

was so long everyone thought it was an *anteater*," Michael laughed. He pulled the photographs out of his backpack and handed them to Daron. "I took the pictures to school and showed them to the secretary. She *recognized* you and called your mom to give her my telephone number. Then your mom called me."

"Now I can show the ant to Dad," said Daron happily. "Thanks, Michael. I guess sometimes people can count on the kindness of a stranger."

大家都以为是食蚁兽呢。"迈克尔笑着说，并从背包里拿出照片，递给达龙。"我把这些照片带到学校给教学秘书看，她认出了你，然后给你妈妈打了电话，并把我的电话号码给了你妈妈。之后，你妈妈给我打了电话。"

"现在我可以把蚂蚁雕塑给爸爸看了。"达龙高兴地说道。"谢谢你，迈克尔。我想说，人间自有真情在啊。"

---

anteater n. 食蚁兽 　　　　　　　　　　　recognize v. 认出；认识

GROWING PAINS IV

9

Carlos's Puzzle

Carlos

Carlos first heard about the *maze* on a cool afternoon in autumn. He liked nothing better than working his way through mazes. In fact, he was an expert at finding the path from beginning to end without getting lost. He knew many of the tricks maze makers used to *disorient* people trying to find the *solution* to their puzzle.

He was in the kitchen creating his special ham sandwich with ham, lettuce, onions, *pickles*, mayo, mustard, and peanut butter,

---

卡洛斯的迷宫

卡洛斯

卡洛斯是在一个凉爽的秋天午后听说迷宫的事的。他最喜欢走迷宫了。其实，他是迷宫专家，能从入口走到出口而不会迷路。他知道设计迷宫的人所用的很多伎俩，那些伎俩使人们难以找到走出迷宫的方向。

卡洛斯正在厨房做特制的火腿三明治时，他妈妈领着阿尔夫走了进来。那个特制的三明治里放了火腿、莴苣、洋葱、腌菜、蛋黄酱、芥末和

---

maze *n.* 迷宫
solution *n.* 解决方法；答案

disorient *v.* 使迷失方向
pickle *n.* 腌菜；泡菜

◆ CARLOS'S PUZZLE

when his mother came in with Alf. Alf barked once, *wagged* his tail, panted at the ham, sat down, and stared up at Carlos.

Alf knew that Carlos would feed him because Carlos always fed him. Carlos did everything for Alf. He filled Alf's bowls, took him for walks, and brushed him when he was matted. He even let Alf sleep beside him. Carlos tossed Alf a small piece of ham and went back to creating his *masterpiece*.

"Have you told Javier yet?" Carlos asked as he folded his sandwich together and took a bite. Javier was Carlos's elder brother, and he had no interest in mazes *whatsoever*.

"Not yet."

花生酱。阿尔夫叫了一声，摇了摇尾巴，眼巴巴地看着火腿，坐下来，又抬头看着卡洛斯。

阿尔夫知道卡洛斯会给它喂食的，因为卡洛斯从不拒绝它的乞求，什么都会为它做。卡洛斯会给阿尔夫的碗里添食，带它出去散步，在给它铺席时还会为它刷毛。他甚至让阿尔夫睡在他身边。卡洛斯扔给阿尔夫一小片火腿，然后又回去继续创造他的杰作了。

"你告诉贾维尔没呢？"卡洛斯边问妈妈，边卷起三明治咬了一口。贾维尔是卡洛斯的哥哥，他对迷宫可是丝毫没有兴趣。

"还没呢。"

---

wag v. 摇动；摇摆（尾巴）　　　　　　masterpiece n. 杰作
whatsoever adv. 任何；丝毫

GROWING PAINS IV

"He'll hate it, you know. If it doesn't have something to do with sports, well, you know what I mean."

"I know he won't be *thrilled*," Mom said as she worked, "but we went to the Sportsplex for him. This time we're doing the maze for you."

Javier

Javier burst into the kitchen as Carlos was putting the dishes into the *dishwasher*. Javi was wet, loud, and invigorated.

"I did it again!" He boomed, as he opened the *refrigerator* door and yanked out the ham. "Make me a ham sandwich, little bro, because I am the man. I am king of the playing field with three base hits and a home run, and I *deserve* a reward."

"他很讨厌走迷宫，你明白我的意思吧，只要是跟他讲无关体育的事，他肯定不高兴。"

"我知道他肯定不会有太大兴趣，"妈妈边做手里的活边说，"但是之前我们已经为他去运动场了。这次他就该为了你一起去迷宫。"

贾维尔

卡洛斯正往洗碗机里放盘子时，贾维尔冲进了厨房。他全身都湿透了，吵吵嚷嚷地，情绪很激动。

"我又创造奇迹了！"他兴奋地打开了冰箱门，把火腿抽了出来。"老弟，给我做个火腿三明治，你哥哥我是英雄。我打了三个安全打，还有一个本垒打，是当之无愧的球王。该给我点奖励。"

---

thrilled *adj.* 欣喜若狂的；非常开心的
refrigerator *n.* 冰箱
dishwasher *n.* 洗碗机
deserve *v.* 值得；应得

◆ CARLOS'S PUZZLE

Carlos considered telling his brother to make his own sandwich when his mother stepped in and told Javier that a big star like him *was* perfectly *capable of* making his own sandwich.

Javier had long ago convinced his younger brother that the things Carlos was good at didn't matter. Carlos got better grades in school, he was an expert chess player and an excellent cook, and he was *brilliant* on the computer, but Javier could not care less.

"Play chess with me, Javier," Carlos would say.

"Chess? Why would I play a boring game like chess when I could be hitting home runs or making *touchdowns*? Let's go out and throw some passes, little bro. Or are you afraid you can't catch anything I might throw your way?"

卡洛斯正想让哥哥自己去做三明治，妈妈就走进来说，像贾维尔这样的大英雄绝对可以自己做三明治。

很早以前，贾维尔就反复告诉弟弟卡洛斯，擅长什么并不重要。其实，卡洛斯的学习成绩比哥哥好，还是下象棋的高手、出色的厨师、电脑精英，但是这些贾维尔一点都不关心。

"贾维尔，咱们下象棋吧，"卡洛斯有时会提出类似的建议。

"下象棋？我去打个全垒打，去来个触地得分多好，干吗要玩那种无聊的游戏？咱们出去练练传球吧，兄弟。还是你害怕我投什么样的球你都接不住？"

---

be capable of 能够
touchdown n. 触地得分

brilliant *adj.* 聪颖的；技艺高超的

GROWING PAINS IV

As Javier ate his sandwich, he learned of the family's trip to the maze. "What's a corn maze?" Javier asked through *a mouthful of* his monster sandwich.

"They're like the mazes in my puzzle books, only 3-D and made by cutting paths through stalks in cornfields," Carlos explained. "Some of them are based on hedge *labyrinth* designs that are hundreds and hundreds of years old. Most of those are easy to walk through." Carlos added. "Some are more modern in design, take up acres of land, and take hours to solve. The one we're going to is supposed to be difficult, but not impossible."

"Sounds *fascinating*," Javier muttered *sarcastically*. "I'll stay with a friend."

贾维尔吃着三明治时，听说了家人要去走迷宫的事。"什么是玉米迷宫？"他满嘴塞着"怪物三明治"问道。

"玉米迷宫就像我字谜书里的迷宫一样，但是实物是三维的，是在玉米秆之间开辟出来的通道，"卡洛斯解释道。"有一些是在篱笆迷宫设计的基础上形成的，篱笆迷宫设计已经有成百上千年的历史了。大部分篱笆迷宫是很容易走出来的，"卡洛斯又说，"有些迷宫设计很现代，占地几公顷，得花几个小时才能走出来。这次我们要走的迷宫就特别难，但是也不是走不出来。"

"听起来真有趣，"贾维尔不无讽刺地嘟哝着，"我还是去朋友那待着吧。"

---

a mouthful of 一口
fascinating *adj.* 让人着迷的；极有吸引力的
labyrinth *n.* 迷宫；迷阵
sarcastically *adv.* 讽刺地；挖苦地

◆ CARLOS'S PUZZLE

"We're all going," his father said firmly, and the boys knew that was that.

The Contest

That night before bed, Carlos came up with a plan and discussed it with Alf.

"So here's my plan, Alf. I'll challenge Javi to a contest. The first one through the maze will be the winner. He's faster, but I'm smarter, so I think I can *beat* him."

Javier was on his bed in the room he and Carlos shared, lost in the tinny music that was leaking from his *headphones*. After a while, he took off the headphones and sat up.

"So, little bro," he said. "If I have to go to this boring maze,

---

"全家人一块儿去，"爸爸很坚决地说。两个孩子都听得出来，没什么商量的余地。

竞赛

那晚卡洛斯上床睡觉前，心生一计，便与阿尔夫商量起来。

"我有个计划，阿尔夫。我要向贾维尔挑战。我们俩谁先走出迷宫，谁就是赢家。他速度比我快，但我比他聪明，我觉得我一定能赢他。"

贾维尔和卡洛斯同住一间卧室。贾维尔正躺在床上享受着音乐，有尖细的音乐声从他的耳机中飘出来。过了一会，他摘掉耳机坐了起来。

"喂，老弟，"他说，"既然我必须得去走无聊的迷宫，不如我们来

---

beat *v.* 打败；战胜   headphone *n.* 双耳式耳机

GROWING PAINS IV

maybe we should make a contest of it to make it more exciting."

Carlos couldn't believe his elder brother was really going to suggest the exact same thing he had just thought. He couldn't have planned it better.

"How about if we say the last one through the maze does all the chores in the house for a month?" Javier continued.

"Hmm... well, okay," Carlos said, trying to sound calm.

"It's a deal then," Javier agreed, and then he laughed.

Carlos and his family piled into the car the next afternoon to drive to the farm with the corn maze. When the people were settled, Alf *crawled* in and *promptly* fell asleep on Carlos's feet.

As Dad drove to the farm, Javier *mentioned* the contest at least ten

---

场比赛吧，还能刺激点。"

卡洛斯无法相信哥哥竟然说出了他的想法。真是人算不如天算啊。

"我说，谁后走出迷宫谁就干一个月的家务活怎么样？"贾维尔继续说道。

"嗯……呃，好吧，"卡洛斯尽量假装平静地答道。

"那就这么定了，"贾维尔说着大笑起来。

第二天下午，卡洛斯和家人依次上车，开向有玉米迷宫的农场。几口人都坐好之后，阿尔夫爬了进来，直扑到卡洛斯大腿上睡起觉来。

爸爸驾车开往农场的途中，贾维尔反反复复地提到这场比赛。他设定

---

crawl *v.* 爬；爬行　　　　　　　　　　promptly *adv.* 立即；马上
mention *v.* 说起；提到

times. He set up rules and *boundaries*. He reminded Carlos to prepare for a very long exhausting month of chores, and told him over and over again that he had no chance of winning.

Carlos didn't answer Javier, not even once.

The Maze

Finally, the family arrived at the *bustling* farm, and Carlos could begin to put an end to Javier's *boasting*. All around them, people were ducking through rows of apple trees carrying paper bags full of apples they had just picked. Still others struggled to carry freshly picked pumpkins to their cars. Javier, Carlos, and Alf *ignored* it all and headed straight for the corn maze.

了比赛规则和惩罚措施，提醒卡洛斯准备好干一个月的家务活，准备好累得筋疲力尽，还一遍遍地说他弟弟没机会获胜。

任凭贾维尔怎么说，卡洛斯一声都没回应。

迷宫

一家人终于到达了熙熙攘攘的农场，卡洛斯也终于不用再忍受贾维尔的自吹自擂了。他们周围的人们都在一排排的苹果树中间穿行，拎着刚摘下来的一兜兜苹果。还有些人费劲地将刚刚摘下的南瓜搬上车。贾维尔、卡洛斯和阿尔夫对这一切视而不见，径直走向玉米迷宫。

---

boundary *n.* 界限；分界线　　　　bustling *adj.* 喧嚷的；繁忙热闹的
boast *v.* 吹嘘；炫耀　　　　　　　ignore *v.* 不顾；忽视

GROWING PAINS IV

At the entrance, the brothers waited their turn as dozens of people stepped into the maze to try their wits at finding its solution. The trio inched closer and closer. Alf *panted* heavily in *anticipation*.

"One, two, three, go!" Javier shouted as soon as it became their turn. Javier took off, *disappearing* quickly onto the first path to the right that cut through the tall, brown corn stalks.

Carlos and Alf did not move. Carlos was thinking, and Alf was waiting.

"Okay Alf," Carlos finally said. "This may be one of the most difficult mazes we've ever tried, but we're clever, and we can beat it. Javi will try to race through the maze, but that's not the way to

---

兄弟俩在迷宫入口处等着轮到他们。有数十人陆续走进迷宫，想在迷宫中试试身手。这三位一步步地挪近迷宫入口。阿尔夫重重地喘息着，焦急地等待行动。

"一、二、三，出发！"一轮到他们，贾维尔就迫不及待地喊道。他率先出发，快速消失在右手边高大的棕色玉米秆间的第一条小路上。

卡洛斯和阿尔夫还在原地。卡洛斯在思索，阿尔夫在等他。

"好了，阿尔夫，"卡洛斯终于开口说道，"这可能是我们走过的最难的迷宫了，但咱们俩这么聪明，肯定能走出去。贾维尔想以速度取胜，

---

pant v. 喘气；喘息 anticipation n. 期望；期盼
disappear v. 消失；不见

◆ CARLOS'S PUZZLE

win. Our *strategy* will be to take our time and think about each of the paths."

Carlos started out with Alf following close behind. He knew the maze was created to make a picture of an apple tree full of fruit from a *billboard* he had seen from the car on his way here. His *experience* with other mazes told him that the maze's start was probably at the base of the tree's trunk, and that there were most likely three possible paths through the maze, each with its own exit at the top of the tree.

It didn't take Carlos long to remember where he had been or to figure out the *correct* paths. After about ten minutes, he knew he had

但在迷宫里靠速度是赢不了的。咱们的策略就是不要着急，每一步都要想清楚再行动。"

卡洛斯出发了，阿尔夫紧跟在他身后。卡洛斯知道这个迷宫被设计成了一棵长满苹果的树，他是在来这的路上在路旁广告牌上看到的。通过以前走迷宫的经验，他凭直觉判断迷宫的出发点很可能是树干处，通过迷宫的路径极可能有三条，每条路径出口都在树冠处。

卡洛斯清楚地记得自己走过的地方，很快就能找到正确的前进路径。过了大约10分钟，他知道自己离出口不远了。他真没想到能够这么快走出迷宫。

strategy *n.* 策略　　　　　　　　　　billboard *n.* 广告牌
experience *n.* 经验　　　　　　　　correct *adj.* 正确的

GROWING PAINS IV

114

◆ CARLOS'S PUZZLE

to be close to the exit. He couldn't believe he had solved the maze so quickly.

Then Carlos came to a dead end. He quickly *retraced* his steps to the *crossroads* where he had taken the left fork and instead took the right. As Carlos moved on, finding his way, turning back, considering his options, he could imagine his brother *thrashing* around in the middle of the maze.

Carlos knew he could easily win this contest now. He was so close to the exit, but he thought he could also hear Javier. Then he chuckled as he heard Javier shouting about how *unfair* it was that he had found himself in a dead end for the third time.

It took Carlos about another five minutes before he saw the exit

---

但是卡洛斯来到了一个死胡同。他快速原路返回，到了他刚才向左转的十字路口，这次改为向右转。卡洛斯一路前进，找准路径，回身重走，思索判断，同时还想象着哥哥疾步奔走于迷宫中间区域的情景。

卡洛斯现在相信自己可以轻松赢得这场比赛。他已经很接近出口，但也听到了附近有贾维尔的声音。然后，卡洛斯听见哥哥叫嚷着自己已经第三次走进同一个死胡同了，这太不公平……他不禁偷笑起来。

卡洛斯又走了5分钟后，看到出口就在眼前。他举起双臂，做出胜利的姿势，开始慢跑向终点，感觉很像电影《洛奇》中的西尔维斯特·史泰

---

retrace *v.* 折回
thrash *v.* 翻来覆去；猛烈摆动

crossroads *n.* 十字路口
unfair *adj.* 不公平的

GROWING PAINS IV

in front of him. Carlos raised his arms in *victory* and started to jog to the finish feeling much like Sylvester Stallone in Rocky. Carlos could hardly believe it. His brother would have to respect his win, and Javier would be doing his chores for a whole month. He felt like he was floating.

The Dilemma

And then Carlos heard Javier again. This time Javier was yelling. He almost sounded *panicked*, but Carlos couldn't be sure. What should he do? What if Javi was trying to trick Carlos to keep him from finishing the maze? Carlos was in a *dilemma*. He could take the final steps to the exit and win and forget about Javi. Or, he could *jeopardize* his win, believe Javi was in trouble, and go back to help him. He could even stay where he was and hope that others in the

---

龙。卡洛斯感觉难以置信。哥哥将对他崇拜得五体投地，然后还得干上一个月的家务活。卡洛斯感觉自己要飘起来了。

抉择

这时，卡洛斯又听见了贾维尔的声音。这一次贾维尔在大喊。他的声音听起来很惊慌，但卡洛斯想不明白了。哥哥在做什么呢？贾维尔是在使用诡计来拖他的后腿吗？卡洛斯不知怎么办才好了。他只要再跑几步，就能到达出口，赢得比赛，不管贾维尔。要么，他就要相信贾维尔遇到了麻烦，回去帮贾维尔，那样就可能丢掉了马上到手的胜利。他甚至可以原地

---

victory *n.* 胜利
dilemma *n.* 困境；（进退两难的）窘境
panic *v.* 惊慌失措；恐慌
jeopardize *v.* 危及；危害

◆ CARLOS'S PUZZLE

maze would help his brother. Carlos stood there and looked down at Alf.

Then Javier started calling for help and saying, "*Seriously*, bro, this is no joke!" Carlos felt Javier must be hurt. He had to do something, so he retraced his steps. He checked the maze paths near Javi's cries, but he didn't find Javier. He then went back to the next *junction* and went right because he had come from the left. As the path *looped* in front of Carlos, he could see Javier's running shoes sticking out from where the corn curved.

Javier looked like he had been trying to pull himself up, but had twisted his ankle badly in a hollow worn in the dirt path. "So, little bro, you got here fast," Javier said, cracking a *grin*. "You must not have been too far ahead of me."

不动,盼着迷宫里的其他人去帮助哥哥。卡洛斯站在那儿,低头看了看阿尔夫。

贾维尔呼救的声音又响了起来。他喊道:"有麻烦了,弟弟,没开玩笑!"卡洛斯感觉贾维尔一定受伤了。他必须得去帮忙,所以他沿原路往回走。他查找了离贾维尔声音很近的迷宫通道,但并没看见贾维尔。他又回到下一个交叉口向右转,因为他刚刚是从左边过来的。卡洛斯面前的路径呈圆形,他看见贾维尔的跑鞋从玉米秆弯下的地方伸出来。

贾维尔看起来像是在挣扎着要站起来,但好像在一条土路的破旧空地上扭伤了脚踝,还伤得很重。"啊,老弟,你来得真快,"贾维尔说着,挤出了一丝笑容,"看来你没比我领先太多。"

---

seriously *adv.* 认真地
loop *v.* 打环;成圈

junction *n.* 交叉路口;汇合处
grin *n.* 露齿的笑;咧嘴的笑

GROWING PAINS IV

"Let's just get you out of here," said Carlos as Javier threw his arm around Carlos's shoulders to *support* his weight. As they walked, Javi *boasted* about how he was running down the path with his mind on the exit so he didn't see the hole. He was going so fast, and it was such a surprise, "Not even Hercules could have stopped himself from going down."

"Crash and burn," Javier said. "It was a fantastic wipeout!"

"I'm glad you weren't too far ahead," he continued. "I tried to walk, but when I tried to put weight on my *ankle*, it just gave out, and I surely wasn't going to hop all the way out."

The Win

"Actually, big bro, I was almost out when I heard you yelling,"

卡洛斯说："我扶你出去吧。"贾维尔把胳膊搭在了卡洛斯肩膀上，让他架着自己走。两个人走着，贾维尔开始吹嘘着自己是如何一心向着出口狂奔才没看见有洞的。他的速度太快了，洞出现得太突然，"就算是赫拉克勒斯（赫拉克勒斯为希腊神话中的大英雄），在跑成那样时也没法停下来。"

"重跌，发烫，"贾维尔说道，"这回可真是伤得不轻！"

"真高兴你没走太远，"贾维尔还在继续说，"我想走来着，但我一想站起来，我的脚踝就撑不住，我肯定也不能一只脚跳着出去啊。"

胜局

"大哥，其实我听见你喊的时候马上就要走出迷宫了，"卡洛斯轻声说道。

---

support *v.* 支持；支撑　　　　　　　　　　　　　　boast *v.* 吹嘘；炫耀
ankle *n.* 踝

Carlos said quietly.

Javier looked up. He could see the exit clearly. His *storytelling* had *distracted* him from the fact that they were still inside the maze and still in the *contest*.

"Well, what do you know?" Javier said, looking his brother in the eye. "It looks like I'm doing chores for a month."

Carlos saw the flash of *pride* in Javier's eyes before it disappeared. That was better than winning.

贾维尔抬起头来，他清楚地看见了出口。他讲故事讲得太投入，都忘了他们此刻还在迷宫里，还在比赛呢。

"对啊，你猜怎么着？"贾维尔说着，看着弟弟的眼睛。"看起来我得干一个月的家务活了。"

卡洛斯看见贾维尔眼中骄傲的神色瞬间不见了，这结果比赢得比赛还开心呢。

---

storytelling *n.* 讲故事   distract *v.* 使分心；分散（注意力）
contest *n.* 比赛   pride *n.* 自豪；得意

GROWING PAINS IV

10

The Mind Game

There once was a very special boy who loved to play games on a computer that sat on his mother's desk. When his mother wasn't using the computer, he was allowed to sit and play for as long as he liked.

When he was playing, the game was like a dream in his mind. He was so *wrapped* up in the game that he didn't know if it was sunny outside. He wouldn't have noticed if a *tornado* was blowing away his house.

头脑游戏

从前有一个非常特别的男孩，他喜欢用妈妈书桌上的电脑玩游戏。他妈妈不用电脑的时候，他就可以坐下来玩，玩多长时间都行。

他玩游戏的时候，感觉就像做梦一样。他玩得非常投入，外面是阴是晴都不知道。就算龙卷风把他的家掀翻了，他都不会注意到。

---

wrap *v.* 包；裹   tornado *n.* 龙卷风

◆ THE MIND GAME

And then one day it happened! He climbed into the chair at his mother's desk. He twisted his neck, *flexed* his fingers, and got ready to play a game, but...

...the *keyboard* was gone!

And so was the monitor and even the mouse.

"Mom!"

The very special boy's *scream* brought his mother and his father running from the kitchen.

"What is it? What happened?" they cried, rushing to his side.

"Mom!" he said, pointing at the desk.

"Look!"

His mother looked. His father looked. "At what, son?" they asked.

然后有一天，真的有事情发生了！他爬到妈妈书桌前的凳子上。他扭了扭脖子，活动活动手指，准备玩游戏，但是……

……键盘不见了。

显示器和鼠标也不见了。

"妈妈！"

听到孩子的尖叫，他的爸爸妈妈赶紧从厨房跑了出来。

"怎么了？发生什么事了？"他们匆忙跑到他身边，大声问道。

"妈妈！"他指着桌子说。

"看哪！"

他的妈妈看着桌子。他的爸爸也看着桌子。"看什么，儿子？"他们问。

---

flex *v.* 活动；屈伸   keyboard *n.* 键盘
scream *n.* 尖叫；尖锐刺耳的声音

GROWING PAINS IV

◆ THE MIND GAME

"There's nothing there."

"I know. I know," he said. "The computer is gone!"

"Oh, is that all," said his mother as she went back to the kitchen.

"The computer is broken. We're having it fixed. It'll be back soon."

"How soon is soon?" the boy cried.

"A week or two," chuckled the father.

It might as well have been a million years. The boy was left alone with nothing to do.

He sat, *forlorn*, at the desk. He stared at the empty place where the screen, keyboard, and mouse used to sit. Now there was nothing except a *raggedy*-paged old book called *Leo the Lop*.

With a deep *sigh*, he opened the book and looked at the words

---

"什么都没有啊。"
"就是说，就是说，"他说，"电脑不见了！"
"啊，这件事啊，"妈妈边说边走回了厨房。
"电脑坏了，我们拿去修了。很快就会拿回来的。"
"很快是多快？"男孩大喊道。
"一两周吧。"父亲咯咯地笑着。
这个男孩度日如年，没人理他，他也不知该干点什么。
他可怜兮兮地坐在桌子前，看着空空的桌子，这里本该放着电脑屏幕、键盘和鼠标。可现在桌上除了一本又破又旧的《耷拉耳朵的小兔力奥》，什么都没有。
他深深地叹了口气，打开书，看着一篇篇的字。他读了几个词，又禁

---

forlorn *adj.* 愁苦的；孤苦伶仃的   raggedy *adj.* 破旧的；脏乱的
sigh *n.* 叹息；叹气

GROWING PAINS IV

spread across the page. He read a few words and then a few more. He was surprised to find that pictures began to form in his mind, just like with the computer game.

Like a river, the pictures from words began to flow through his mind as he read the *wonderful* story.

He read that book and another and another. He read stories about *bunnies*, *butterflies*, and bears.

In time, the computer was returned. But the very special boy now had a very special game that didn't need a mouse or a keyboard.

For from books come dreams, and from dreams come magical tomorrows.

不住继续读下去。他吃惊地发现，这些词跟电脑游戏一样在他的脑海中形成了一幅幅图画。

他读着这个精彩的故事，感觉字词形成的图画就像是一条小河在头脑中流淌开来。

他读完了这本，又接着读了好几本。他读了小兔子的故事，蝴蝶的故事，还有熊的故事。

电脑准时拿回来了。但是这个特别的男孩现在喜欢上了一个无需鼠标键盘的非常特殊的游戏。

因为书籍点燃了梦想，而梦想点亮了神奇的未来。

---

wonderful *adj.* 精彩的
butterfly *n.* 蝴蝶

bunny *n.* 兔子

◆ THE MIND GAME

GROWING PAINS IV

11

Ants in My Bed

Introduction

When I was nine years old, I spent the summer with my great-grandmother. Gram lived in a large, gray, cedar shakes house at the *seashore*. I stayed in the yellow bedroom, where my father slept as a boy. The room's window faced the ocean, and the sound of the waves breaking against the shore always helped me sleep. At least it did until the ants *showed up* a few weeks into my visit.

床上的蚂蚁

引子

我九岁那年,暑假是在曾祖母家度过的。她(我叫她太姥姥)住在海边一座杉木屋顶的灰色大房子里。我住在一间黄色卧室里,这是我爸爸小时候住的地方。房间窗户面向大海,我常在海浪拍岸的节奏中入眠。我刚到这的前几周一直是这样,但后来有了蚂蚁,一切就变样了。

---

seashore *n.* 海岸　　　　　　　　　　　show up 显现出来

I spent the first few weeks exploring the sea and saving the lives of some horseshoe *crabs*. I also had been busy riding the old bike Gram's friend, Jim, gave me. I was not allowed to ride very far on the weekends because the town and beach became crowded with tourists. During the week, I explored as I pleased.

Jim usually *dropped by* in the mornings to eat breakfast with Gram and me. Sometimes he'd stick around to help Gram with big *chores* around the house. Other times he would take me down to the shore and teach me how to make sand castles.

Sand Castles

I always looked for different ways to make my castles special. I

我花了几周时间来探索大海的秘密，还救起了不少马蹄蟹。我也经常骑太姥姥的朋友吉姆送给我的旧自行车。周末的时候，大人们不让我骑得太远，因为镇里和海滩上满是游客，人山人海。只要不是周末，我就可以尽情地去探索了。

早上，吉姆经常过来坐坐，与太姥姥和我一起吃早饭。有时，他还会多待上一会儿，帮太姥姥做些重家务活。没有重活的时候，他就会带我去海滩，教我怎样做沙堡。

沙堡

我总是尝试各种各样的方法来做出独特的沙堡。我用各种尺寸的杯

---

crab *n.* 蟹；螃蟹　　　　　　　　drop by 顺道拜访；造访
chore *n.* 琐事；家务活

GROWING PAINS IV

used varying sizes of cups, buckets, spoons, shovels, garden tools, and toys to create *wondrous* castles big enough for sea gulls or small enough for ants to march through. Sometimes I made castles, hoping the ants in my bed would make it their new home. I settled for placing toy people in and around the castle once it was finished.

To make a sand castle, first I would smooth out a flat *surface* to support it. Next, I would dig up very wet sand, but not dripping wet, and pack it tight into a bucket mold. Then I would gently tap the sand out to form the base of my castles.

I added details by pressing wet sand together in my hands and smoothing it up into lookout towers, *balconies*, and *protective* walls. Sometimes I dug a deep moat, or ditch, around the castle and filled

---

子、小桶、勺子、铲子、园艺工具，还有各种玩具来做出许多奇妙的沙堡，大的大到能容海鸥飞过，小的小到只有蚂蚁可以通行。有时，我做沙堡的目的是希望我床上的蚂蚁可以搬到它们的沙堡新家。每建好一个沙堡，我还会把一些玩具人物摆在沙堡内外。

我建沙堡时，会先摊开一块足以建堡的平地。然后，挖起很湿的沙子（很湿但不能滴水），再将湿沙填进小桶模具，压实。接下来，就要将沙子轻拍出来，作为建堡的地基。

至于其他需要点缀的细节，我会将湿沙捏紧、拍平，然后就可以建起瞭望塔、阳台，或是防御墙。有时我还会在沙堡周围挖一条壕沟，里面注满水。

---

wondrous adj. 奇异的；令人惊叹的
balcony n. 阳台

surface n. 表面
protective adj. 防护的

◆ ANTS IN MY BED

GROWING PAINS IV

it with water. I often dripped watery sand on the edges to make fancy *designs* along the roof and down the walls. As a final touch, I would add shells, driftwood, seaweed, and sea glass that I had collected with Jim earlier in the morning.

Sea Glass

Sometimes Jim took me with him to walk down the beach and look for gifts from the sea. Jim called the *treasures* we found "gifts" because once in a great while he would find something very interesting. He had found pieces of metal or wood from ships, teeth from a big fish, and even coins. Jim *especially* liked to find sea glass, which he collected.

在堡顶和墙周的边沿,我常加上滴水的湿沙,形成华丽的装饰。最后的点睛之笔,就是添加上我和吉姆早上捡来的那些贝壳、浮木、海草和海玻璃。

海玻璃

有时,吉姆会领我在海边走,寻找大海馈赠的礼物。吉姆有时看到某样东西会突然童心大发,所以他把我们找到的宝贝叫"礼物"。他曾经发现过船上掉下的金属条或木头块,大鱼的牙齿,甚至还有硬币,但他收集最多的,是他最喜欢的海玻璃。

---

design *n.* 设计(样式)   treasure *n.* 珍宝
especially *adv.* 尤其;特别

◆ ANTS IN MY BED

Jim told me sea glass is broken glass that has been worn smooth over time by the wind, waves, and sand. This makes the sharp edges rounded so they feel nice to hold. The little pieces of glass glowed *brilliantly* when the sun shined into them. Jim found most of his sea glass during low *tide* after a storm *churned up* the ocean. He said most of what washed in with the tide was from the early 1900s when people threw glass overboard from *steamboats*.

When I went with Jim to look for gifts we would sort through what we had collected before I built my sand castle that day.

Early in my visit, I had learned to ask Gram for the local tide reports in the mornings. She explained how I could listen for them on the radio, or read them in the local newspaper, too. I wanted to find

---

吉姆告诉我，海玻璃本是玻璃碎片，但是在被风、海浪和沙子长时间打磨后变得很平滑。这样，原来的碎片尖角被磨圆了，拿在手里很舒服。阳光照过来，这一小块玻璃就会闪闪发光。吉姆的大部分海玻璃都是在风暴席卷海岸之后，海潮退去时发现的。他说，20世纪初，轮船上的人们向海里扔玻璃，现在被浪潮卷过来的，就是当时人们扔的玻璃。

我和吉姆一边寻找"礼物"，一边将我们捡来的东西分类存放，准备等再建沙堡的时候用。

我刚到太姥姥家的时候，问过太姥姥在哪可以得到早间的潮汐预报。她告诉我收音机里和当地的报纸上都有。我想知道什么时间最利于寻找海

---

brilliantly *adv.* 非常好地；出色地
churn up 搅拌

tide *n.* 潮汐；潮水
steamboat *n.* 汽船；汽艇

GROWING PAINS IV

out the best times for finding sea glass and for building my castles.

Much to my *dismay*, during high tide the incoming waves *destroyed* my castles—washed them right into the sea. Gram said that the tides, or the *ebb* and flow of seawater, is caused by the attraction, or pull, of the sun and moon. About every 12 hours I would say goodbye to that day's castle. Then I could start all over again, building different castles and trying out new ways to shape and *decorate* them.

Visitors

I was having a terrific summer. Gram gave me easy chores like making my bed, washing the dishes, and sweeping her porches. I

玻璃，什么时间最利于建沙堡。

在满潮时，卷起的海浪会使我的沙堡化为乌有，葬身大海，这让我很是沮丧。太姥姥说，潮汐是指海水涨潮或退潮，是因为太阳和月亮的引力形成的。每过大约12个小时，我就要对当天建好的沙堡说再见。然后我从头再来，建起新的沙堡，再试着用不同的方法进行装点。

不速之客

我这个暑假过得棒极了。太姥姥让我做的事都很简单，比如整理床铺、洗碗，还有打扫门廊。大部分时间我都是自由自在的，可以去码头之

---

dismay *n.* 哀伤；焦虑　　　　　destroy *v.* 摧毁；破坏
ebb *n.* 退潮　　　　　　　　　decorate *v.* 装饰

◆ ANTS IN MY BED

was usually free to *roam* my part of the beach between two jetties, ride my bicycle, read books, make friends with visiting children, or explore the shops in town.

I had just one problem, and I didn't know how to solve it. I had ants in my bed. The ants didn't actually live in my bed. They just crawled across it. I seemed to be an *obstacle* in their path. Instead of going around me, they climbed over me! I wasn't sleeping well thinking of *creepy*, crawly ants skittering across me in the night.

I didn't want to smash or stomp or *spray* the ants. I just wanted them to crawl somewhere else. I went to the town's library and asked the librarian where I could check out books about ants to find

间的海滩上闲逛——那里有我的领地；可以骑自行车、读书、和参观的孩子们交朋友，也可以去镇里的商店看看都有些什么。

只有一件麻烦事让我束手无策——那就是床上的蚂蚁。蚂蚁没有在我的床上安家，只是从床上经过，我倒成了它们行程上的障碍。它们从不绕着我走，而是直接从我身上爬过去！我每晚想到那些蚂蚁在我身上爬来爬去，就觉得汗毛都竖起来了，根本没办法睡安稳。

我不想去拍死或是踩死这些蚂蚁，也不想用杀虫剂杀死它们，我只是想让它们去别处爬。我去了镇里的图书馆，问管理员哪里有关于蚂蚁的书——找到书就能解决这个麻烦了。那里有很多关于蚂蚁的书，我翻看了

roam *v.* 漫步；闲逛　　　　　　　　obstacle *n.* 障碍；障碍物
creepy *adj.* 令人毛骨悚然的　　　　　spray *v.* 喷；喷洒

GROWING PAINS IV

a solution to my dilemma. I looked through many, checked out four, and headed back to Gram's house.

Ants

As I read, I learned that ants live in *colonies*, which may exist for many years. Each colony has at least one queen that lays eggs. In about 25 days, the eggs turn into *larvae*. In another 10 days, the larvae make white cocoons to cover themselves. Inside the cocoons, the larvae turn into ant-shaped pupae. Altogether, it takes almost 60 days for a new worker ant to be born. In just one colony, thousands of worker ants find food, build nests, and take care of the queen and her young. The book said ants eat a variety of food such as *insects*,

---

不少，最后借了四本，就回家去了。

蚂蚁

通过阅读，我知道了蚂蚁在蚁群中生活，这个现象可能已经存在许多年了。每个蚁群有至少一个蚁后负责产卵。25天以后，卵形成幼虫。再过10天，幼虫吐出白色的茧将自己包裹起来，并在茧内变成蚂蚁形状的蛹。在经过共计60天左右的周期后，一只工蚁就出生了。在一个蚁群中，有上千只工蚁负责觅食、建巢，照顾蚁后和幼仔。书中说，蚂蚁是杂食动物，它们吃昆虫、种子，也吃花蜜（植物分泌的甜味汁液）。

---

colony *n.* 群体；集群　　　　　　　　　　　larvae *n.* 幼虫
insect *n.* 昆虫

seeds, and nectar, which is the sweet juice plants produce.

I found out that ants have three parts—the head, the *thorax*, and the *abdomen*. The head contains the brain, two eyes, the jaws, and the *antennae*. The eyes of an ant are called compound eyes because each eye is actually made up of many eyes. The jaws of an ant open and close like scissors. Ants use their antennae to hear, taste, smell, and *communicate* by touching each other.

This was all pretty interesting, but I still didn't know how to get the ants off my bed.

As I kept reading, I learned the thorax contains three pairs of legs. At the end of each leg is a sharp claw that helps the ant to climb up walls. An ant has such strong legs that if a man could run as fast as

---

我还知道了蚂蚁身体分为三个部分——头部、胸部和腹部。头部包括大脑、两只眼睛、下颌和触角。蚂蚁的眼睛叫作复眼，因为它们每只眼睛实际都是由多个眼睛组成的。蚂蚁的下颌一开一合，就像剪刀一样。它们用触角来听声音、尝味道、嗅气味，也用触角彼此交流。

这些知识都很有趣，但我还是不知道怎样赶走床上的蚂蚁。
我继续读下去，知道了蚂蚁的胸部有六条腿。在每条腿的末端是锋利的爪，可以用来爬墙。蚂蚁的腿十分有力。如果人类能和蚂蚁跑得一样快，其速度就足以媲美一匹赛马。

---

thorax *n.* 胸部
antennae *n.* 触角；触须
abdomen *n.* 腹部
communicate *v.* 交流；沟通

GROWING PAINS IV

an ant, he'd be able to *keep up with* a racehorse.

The abdomen contains the stomach. Between the thorax and the abdomen are one or two bumps called nodes. Ants do not breathe as we do because they do not have lungs. They have holes all over their body, which take in oxygen and send out carbon dioxide.

Finally, I came to a part in one book that talked about how ants lay *scented* trails to find the way from their nest to food and back. I decided that the ants in my room must have laid a scented trail that went across my bed.

I knew I had to find their nest. I'd read it could be under a stone, under a log, or in a garden. Worker ants often come into houses looking for *crumbs* of food, especially sweet things. I thought I had been careful eating in my room, but Gram's *yummy* cookies,

---

蚂蚁腹部是胃所在的地方，在其胸部与腹部之间有一两处突起叫作节。蚂蚁与人类的呼吸方式不同，因为蚂蚁没有肺。它们全身是孔，可以用孔吸进氧气，排出二氧化碳。

最后，我在一本书里读到蚂蚁怎样在路途上留下气味来记住路线——从这条路它们就可以在巢穴与食物之间往返。我相信，房间里的蚂蚁一定是在我的床上留下了有特殊气味的路线。

我知道得找到它们的巢穴。书上说，巢穴可能在石头下、木头下，或是花园里。工蚁进入房间，通常是为了寻找食物碎屑，特别是甜食。我觉得我在房间吃东西时很注意卫生，但是太姥姥做的美味甜饼干，特别是那

---

keep up with 跟上
crumb n. 食物碎屑
scented adj. 芳香的；清香的
yummy adj. 美味的

◆ ANTS IN MY BED

GROWING PAINS IV

especially her peanut butter ones, did crumble. Ants carry food, such as cookies, to the nest after *softening* it with *saliva* and biting off a piece. I read that an ant can carry 20 to 50 times its body weight. I weighed 75 pounds. That meant if I was as strong as an ant, I could carry from 1,500 to 3,750 pounds!

The Search

I tried to follow the ants that were crawling into my room, to find where they were coming from and where they were going. I discovered they were finding crumbs on my floor and in my bed. Then, they were carrying the crumbs near the window, where they escaped between the woodwork and the wall. I went outside and tried to find them coming out of the house. I saw many ants, but none were carrying crumbs of cookies. Maybe they lived under the

---

些花生酱饼干，确实有饼干渣掉在地上。蚂蚁会用唾液将饼干一类的食物软化，再一点点咬下来，搬运到巢穴。我在书中读到，蚂蚁能搬运相当于自身体重20至50倍的东西。我的体重是75磅，这就是说，如果我像蚂蚁那么强壮，我就能搬动1500磅到3750磅的重物！

搜寻

我努力地寻找蚂蚁在我房间里爬行的路线，看看它们是从哪儿来、到哪儿去的。我发现它们是在房间地板上和我的床上发现饼干碎屑的。然后，它们把碎屑搬到窗边，再从木头和墙的缝隙间钻出去。我走出房间，希望能看到蚂蚁从屋里出来。我确实看到了很多蚂蚁，但是没有蚂蚁搬运着饼干渣。说不定它们就住在房子下面！说不定它们就住在墙里！我觉得

---

soften *v.* （使）变软   saliva *n.* 唾液；口水

◆ ANTS IN MY BED

house! Maybe they lived in the walls! I decided I needed to *confess* to Gram.

I told Gram about the ants and even about the cookie crumbs. I also said that I did not want to hurt them, I just wanted to get them off my bed. I asked Gram if I could use her *vacuum cleaner* to sweep up the crumbs in my room.

I also asked if I could move the bed. I cleaned my room, changed the sheets, and *scooted* my bed closer to the window. I vowed not to eat cookies in my room anymore. I wondered if this would end my ant problems.

As I lay in my bed that night, I thought about all of the ants that had been crawling in my room. I decided to ask Gram if I could put

---

我必须要向太姥姥把蚂蚁的事说出来了。

我对太姥姥讲了蚂蚁的事，还有饼干渣我也说了。我还说不想伤害蚂蚁，只是不想让它们在床上爬。我向太姥姥借吸尘器想打扫一下房间里的饼干渣，还对她说我想把床换个位置。然后，我就打扫了房间，换了床单，还把床推得离窗户更近了。我发誓，再也不在房间里吃饼干了。就是不知道这一切努力能不能解决我的蚂蚁问题。

那天晚上，我躺在床上，想着之前在我房间里爬来爬去的蚂蚁。我决定去问问太姥姥，可不可以在卧室窗外的地上放些蜂蜜来喂养蚂蚁，毕竟，是我切断了它们的食物来源。我闭上眼睛，不由自主地笑了起来。就

---

confess *v.* 坦白；承认
scoot *v.* 急走；疾行

vacuum cleaner 真空吸尘器

GROWING PAINS IV

some honey on the ground under my bedroom window to feed the ants since I'd taken away their food *source*. I closed my eyes with a smile on my face. Then I heard some strange noises outside my window. I looked out and saw winged things flying around in the *moonlight*. These black, flying things seemed to *swoop* back and forth from the house. Oh, no! We have bats in the Attic!

Appendix

Gram's Peanut Butter Cookies

Ingredients:

1 cup brown sugar	1 cup shortening or butter
3/4 cup white sugar	1 cup peanut butter
2 eggs	1 teaspoon vanilla
1/4 teaspoon salt	2 teaspoons baking soda

在这时，我听到窗外有奇怪的响声。我向窗外望去，只见夜色中有些带翅膀的东西在空中盘旋。那些黑色的飞行物好像就在我们房子的周围来回猛冲。哦，不会吧！我们的阁楼里有蝙蝠！

附录

太姥姥的花生酱饼干

原料：

1杯红糖	1杯起酥油或黄油
3/4杯白糖	1杯花生酱
2个鸡蛋	1茶匙香草精
1/4茶匙盐	2茶匙小苏打

---

source *n.* 来源
swoop *v.* 猛冲；俯冲
moonlight *n.* 月光；月色
appendix *n.* 附录

◆ ANTS IN MY BED

2 cups flour   1/4 cup sugar (to dip fork)

Instructions:

1. Preheat oven to 350 degrees F.

2. Mix together the brown and white sugars, butter or *shortening*, and peanut butter until *creamy*.

3. Stir in the 2 eggs and mix well.

4. Stir in the *vanilla*.

5. Mix the salt and baking soda into the flour. Slowly add the flour mixture to the *peanut* butter mixture, stirring as you add it.

6. Roll into golf-ball-sized balls.

7. Press onto a cookie sheet with a sugar-coated fork. (Dip a fork

---

2杯面粉   1/4杯糖（用来蘸叉子）

操作步骤：

1. 将锅加热到350华氏度（约为176摄氏度）。

2. 将红糖、白糖、黄油或起酥油与花生酱混合，搅拌至糊状。

3. 放入2个鸡蛋，搅拌均匀。

4. 加入香草精并搅拌。

5. 将盐和小苏打加入面粉中。慢慢地将混合好的面粉倒入混合好的花生酱中，一边倒一边搅拌。

6. 将混合物做成高尔夫球大小的球状。

7. 用蘸了糖的叉子将其压进饼干薄板中。（先用叉子蘸上白糖，再

---

shortening *n.* 起酥油   creamy *adj.* 含乳脂多的；光滑细腻的
vanilla *n.* 香草   peanut *n.* 花生

GROWING PAINS IV

into white sugar and press down on the cookie.)

8. Bake at 350 degrees for 8 to 10 minutes.

9. Cool on a rack. Yields about three dozen cookies.

NOTE: Please have an adult help you any time you use an *electric mixer* or the *oven*.

用来压饼干）。

8. 在350华氏度下烘烤8至10分钟。

9. 在架子上冷却。这样就做出了大约三打（三打为36个）饼干。

注意：在使用电动搅拌仪或电烤箱时，一定要有成人在旁指导。

---

electric *adj.* 用电的；电动的　　　　　　mixer *n.* 搅拌机；混合器
oven *n.* 烤箱